Advance praise for Mary Hayes Grieco and

unconditional
FORGIVENESS

"This is a beautiful and wise book about one of the greatest and most challenging spiritual paths: the practice of forgiveness. This clear and gentle guide offers the promise of release from wounds both small and large, the creation of genuine emotional freedom, and the opening of the heart to be able to give and receive love. Who would not want that?"

DR. HENRY EMMONS, author of *The Chemistry of Joy*

"I love her work, wisdom, and humor."

ANNE LAMOTT, author of *Traveling Mercies* and *Plan B*

"A book on the art of forgiving might not sound like a snappy read, but you would be wrong. Mary Hayes Grieco's writing is fresh, forthright, and user-friendly. Having experienced the efficacy of this work from the inside out, I can tell you its truth rolls over you in ever-bigger waves."

MIKE FINLEY, forgiveness workshop participant

"What a simple way to make important changes! I have worked for so many years in the field of recovery, trying to help people with forgiveness, and indeed apply it to my own life. Mary's training gave me new tools and fresh ideas that I had not experienced before."

SR. EILEEN FAHEY, founder and former CEO of Aiséirí Treatment Centre, Tipperary, Republic of Ireland

"Mary... is a gifted and inspiring presenter with a wealth of knowledge. In the training she presented for the European Branch of the American Counseling Association, our members gained valuable skills to use in their counseling practices. It was a very enriching experience, personally and professionally, and I am using my new knowledge already."

FRANKIE NIELSEN, EdD, former president of EB-ACA

"This forgiveness process is the most effective tool I have to use in my psychotherapy practice. For many of my patients this process has healed wounds they felt couldn't be healed— they are amazed by the results."

MARY CONNER, MA, LP

"I have experienced the power of this forgiveness model, both personally, in a workshop, and professionally, with people in recovery at Hazelden's Dan Anderson Renewal Center. *Unconditional Forgiveness* details just how the Eight Steps to Freedom can support any Twelve-Step program of recovery. Mary Hayes Grieco is a wise, accessible guide through this powerful model of emotional healing."

JOANN CAMPBELL-RICE, spiritual care coordinator, Hazelden's Dan Anderson Renewal Center

"Mary teaches a forgiveness process that is simple yet powerful in healing long-standing hurts and resentments. She is a results-oriented teacher who brings wisdom and humor to her work. I have personally benefited from Mary's method, and I recommend this forgiveness process to anyone who wants to lead a more loving life."

REV. ANN ROMANCZUK, Unitarian Universalist minister and chaplain

"I have consumed every type of personal growth material over the years, from Anthony Robbins to fire walking, and I think of Mary's work as the most gentle and on-target of them all. It eliminates the heavy load the recipient has been carrying for decades, and the magic of the soul is released with the miracle of forgiveness!"
CARL GEORGE, CEO, Rainwater LLC

"Mary's unique approach creates immediate relief in a natural way—it is despair repair! This powerhouse tool transforms people's lives in a very short amount of time, and it is a must-have tool for anyone who is letting go of their past and is ready to attract wealth. Forgiveness removes stuck energy and paves the way for the prospect of good fortune."
MICKEY MIKEWORTH, financial advisor, CEO, Rich Chicks

"This training hit the mark by addressing a need that we have not been able to address by other means. It got to the gut-level pain people are experiencing in our corporate restructuring, in a way that was emotionally safe for everyone. The forgiveness techniques are very helpful to guide people toward positive attitudes and outcomes."
DEBBIE JORGENS, career and employee development, Thrivent Financial

"Forgiveness can feel so foreign. Even though we sense deep inside that freedom lies on the other side of forgiveness, we can't quite seem to get there on our own. In *Unconditional Forgiveness*, Mary Hayes Grieco takes us gently by the hand, never leaving our side, as we walk through the eight-step process that has healed thousands. As we close the book, we are, at long last, free, healthy,

and whole. And life can begin afresh.
I highly recommend this important book."

JANET CONNER, author of *Writing Down Your Soul* and *My Soul Pages*

"In *Unconditional Forgiveness* Mary Hayes Grieco's passion and expertise help the reader with one of the most difficult but worthwhile processes in life—forgiveness. She wisely explains why it is in our best interest to forgive, and how to do it. I found this book personally helpful."

DR. ROBERT BISWAS-DIENER, Positive Psychology LLC, author of *Happiness*

"Mary Hayes Grieco's book offers us engaging, story-driven science and a straightforward approach to relieving emotional pain. It's a must-have for anyone interested in living a longer, better life."

DAN BUETTNER, author of the *New York Times* bestseller *The Blue Zones* and *Thrive*

"When it comes to teaching people how to forgive, Mary Hayes Grieco is the master! With her depth and breadth of insight into this difficult topic, and her warm, creative teaching style, I have witnessed Mary successfully lead group after group of individuals from their starting point of pain and limitation into the new territory and the wider vista that opens up with the liberating experience of forgiveness."

SUE PAISLEY, training department, HealthEast Care System, St. Paul, MN

unconditional FORGIVENESS

A Simple and Proven Method to Forgive Everyone and Everything

Mary Hayes Grieco

ATRIA PAPERBACK
New York London Toronto Sydney New Delhi

BEYOND WORDS
Hillsboro, Oregon

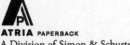
ATRIA PAPERBACK
A Division of Simon & Schuster, Inc.
1230 Avenue of the Americas
New York, NY 10020

BEYOND WORDS
20827 N.W. Cornell Road, Suite 500
Hillsboro, Oregon 97124-9808
503-531-8700 / 503-531-8773 fax
www.beyondword.com

The information contained in this book is intended to be educational and not for diagnosis, prescription, or treatment of any health disorder whatsoever. This information should not replace consultation with a competent healthcare professional. The content of this book is intended to be used as an adjunct to a rational and responsible healthcare program prescribed by a professional healthcare practitioner. The author and publisher are in no way liable for any misuse of the material.

Managing editor: Lindsay S. Brown
Editor: Emily Han
Copyeditor: Ashley Van Winkle
Proofreader: Linda M. Meyer
Design: Devon Smith
Illustrator: Lois Rhomberg
Composition: William H. Brunson Typography Services

First Atria Paperback/Beyond Words trade paperback edition December 2011

ATRIA PAPERBACK and colophon are trademarks of Simon & Schuster, Inc.
Beyond Words Publishing is a division of Simon & Schuster, Inc.

For more information about special discounts for bulk purchases,
please contact Simon & Schuster Special Sales at 1-866-506-1949 or
business@simonandschuster.com.

The Simon & Schuster Speakers Bureau can bring authors to your live event.
For more information or to book an event, contact the Simon & Schuster Speakers
Bureau at 1-866-248-3049 or visit our website at www.simonspeakers.com.

Manufactured in the United States of America

10 9 8 7 6 5 4 3 2 1

Library of Congress Cataloging-in-Publication Data

Hayes Grieco, Mary.
    Unconditional forgiveness : a simple and proven method to forgive everyone and everything /
Mary Hayes Grieco.
        p. cm.
    1. Forgiveness.   I. Title.
    BF637.F67H39   2011
    158.2—dc23

                                                                                    2011028419

ISBN: 978-1-58270-299-5
ISBN: 978-1-4516-2643-8 (eBook)

The corporate mission of Beyond Words Publishing, Inc.: *Inspire to Integrity*

I wrote this book for all of us.
It is dedicated to freeing the joy of the human spirit.
Let's rock the planet with love!

Contents

Acknowledgments

Many thanks to my teachers: Dr. Edith Stauffer, Dr. Roberto Assagioli, and the spiritual masters with whom I walk in a lifelong path of mutual devotion and service. Deep gratitude to my husband of thirty years, Fred Grieco, a master in his own way.

Thanks to my mighty companions and helpmates on the journey: Ann Scott Dumas, Lois Rhomberg, Jamie Reich, Annette Rondano, Terre Thomas, Marci Heerman, Carl George, Deanna Rose Hopper, Kinshasha Kambui, Mary Conner, "The Peeps" (Teesie Vallero, Sue Paisley, Kate Pfaffinger, Deb Magnuson and Paul Kirst, Mary Flood-Maneely, Mary Roettger, Kiersten Dahl-Shetka, Anna McDonagh, John Larsen, and Mike Stewart) . . . and the rest of you—you know who you are.

Thanks to my family, Hayes and Grieco . . . for showing me unconditional love and forgiveness so many times. And a special thanks to my parents, Bill Hayes and Joan Hayes, who infused our home with these qualities.

Thanks to the loving volunteers: Barb Crist, Diana Knoebel, Joy Anderson, Sue Scholten, Rene Erikson, Linda LaBarre, Chris

LaBarre, Joanne Lieske, Angie Ryan, Kit Naylor, Betsy Peterson, Tracey Rush, John Mischke, Lynn Marrs, Teresa Saracino, and Jim Albani—for helping me along.

Thanks to Michael Kelberer, who believed in my writing twenty years ago and helped me get started. Thanks to all the good people at Beyond Words Publishing, my partners in transformation, for their insight, caring, and high integrity in crafting a book with a universal language. I enjoyed our warm and respectful collaboration.

Big thanks to Laurie Harper, my agent, who has shrewd instincts about books and the publishing industry and a warm, supportive heart for her author—a great combination. And to Bonnie Harris of Wax Marketing, who is so cool in the coolest way.

Thanks to everyone who has ever attended a course or workshop, for teaching me more about unconditional forgiveness and the beauty and resilience of the human spirit.

Introduction

A Passion for Freedom

I am writing this at midsummer and I am enjoying a taste of freedom. Newly released from the duty of getting my daughter up and out for school, as she is happily ensconced at her best friend's house for the weekend, I am free to slouch around at my cabin with my quiet husband, my best friend. It's a rare form of freedom when there is neither work nor a child to take care of, and I love it. Crickets and birds sing outside in the twilight, and the green world presses in all around, protectively. I am aware of savoring an empty feeling inside—a good emptiness. My mind is quiet, my body is relaxed, and there is nothing compelling me into action. I can actually do whatever I want to, and I am grateful tonight for this rare conjunction of peace and freedom, internal and external. The world's all right, I say.

I can remember going away for a weekend break to a cabin, about twenty-five years ago, and finding myself utterly incapable of relaxing or enjoying myself, because there was so much unrest inside me. I paced around like a cagey cat with a twitchy tail, and I argued with myself about smoking another cigarette or eating something. I worried about whether my boyfriend was being faithful. I felt guilty about not calling my parents lately, but couldn't stand them or myself. I wanted to write a book, but I had nothing to say. I wondered what to do with myself and if I would ever amount to anything. I tossed and turned with nameless anxiety... in other words, I suffered. I was in a chronic state of suffering over nothing and everything, ill at ease within my own skin. It's hard to think I was even the same person who is sitting here today. Maybe this is just the natural difference between being fifty-five instead of thirty, but I also want to believe that it has to do with the fact that I've been on a journey of spiritual growth and self-healing for a long time. I've been consciously whacking, chipping, digging out, and polishing off my emotional issues, layer upon layer, for many years now. I daresay I'm actually scraping the bottom of the barrel! I'm starting to feel happy and free on a deep level.

In the spring of 1986, when I was thirty-two, I met a woman who had peace and freedom shining out of her like sunlight. Dr. Edith Stauffer was seventy-seven when I met her at a women's retreat in a Unity Church, and in that meeting, I immediately recognized the masterful soul who would soon become my most important life teacher. Edith was living and teaching her principles of Unconditional Love and Forgiveness, a synthesis of her spiritual studies and over thirty-five years of experience as a psychotherapist. With this elegant reduction of her great knowledge into a few universal principles and a coherent step-by-step way to heal the wounded psyche, she offered me the key to happiness, freedom, and my own future life's work. I was taken by the truth and simplicity in her definitions: *unconditional love* is a mental attitude to see the inherent good in any person or situation. It is also a Divine Force, an impersonal form of love that extends itself freely to all without limits, expectations, conditions, or demands—a transformative Force of healing and blessing in the Universe. *Forgiveness* is canceling or releasing an expectation that is causing one to suffer. "It's not hard to forgive," Edith always said. "You just need to know *how*." Even back in the 1980s, a time when a lot of people were doing long stints of therapy, she made the stunning declaration: "It is an old notion of psychotherapy that emotional healing has to take a long time. An effective method of forgiveness is the key." The emotional healings that took place in Edith's workshops were indeed astonishing in their swiftness and their sense of completeness, and I was soon motivated to learn how to use this practical tool to help myself and others.

Edith inspired me by living a masterful life: she worked long and steadily into her advanced years, doing work that ended suffering and uplifted humanity—and she had a rich and love-filled personal life too. Over the course of her extensive career, she was a professor at a university and the director of two different counseling centers and a mountaintop retreat center. At sixty, she traveled for twenty-five years around the United States and in many other countries, teaching people how to forgive and making friends wherever she went. She also wrote and self-published a book about her life's work titled *Unconditional Love and Forgiveness*, which contained her forgiveness steps, oddly seasoned with a mix of esoteric wisdom and her own practical native Texan "horse sense." (You can still find copies of this book, in a number of languages, on the internet.)

By the time I met Edith, she had become a walking treasure chest full of miracle stories from the thousands of people she had healed and helped through the power of her Unconditional Love and Forgiveness method. Her life was a lush garden of fulfillment, the landscape peopled with children and great-grandchildren, a long and loving marriage, financial independence, and admiring students from all around the world. I watched Edith hold the reins of her life with a firm but supple grip, and I noted how she was quick to express a passionate opinion and just as quick to laugh and let it go completely. Despite all the riches surrounding her, I was struck by a certain positive emptiness within her, like a flute through which Spirit plays a continuous, gentle song.

I invite you to picture her as I have known her. . . . On the day we meet at a women's retreat, she is walking down a hill on a forest path. The fresh spring sunlight shines on her snow-white hair, and her tiny feet in old-lady shoes tread along resolutely in a way that is rare in someone who is seventy-seven. She walks tall even though she doesn't even make five feet. She smiles softly at the beauty around her, yet I see that she carries a will of steel.

She is teaching a workshop, where she has just stood for an hour paying perfect attention to a tormented woman who was sexually abused by her grandfather. At the end of the session, the woman is spent and utterly peaceful. Her beauty, veiled an hour ago, is startling. She looks at Edith worshipfully, but Edith smiles with gentle detachment, pats her mildly, and says, "There. Now that's all fixed up." She says it like she has just mended a broken fence, not the life of a human being. We take our coffee break; the world is restored one degree closer to wholeness.

It is the end of a successful workshop day, early on in our relationship. Edith and I are in our room, settling down for the night. I watch with amusement as she removes her stockings in the same manner that I do: standing up, balancing on one foot like a yogi, instead of sitting down to take them off. "I like to keep challenging myself physically in all the little ways I can, so I don't grow old. . . ." She has the mindset of a master, and it manifests all day long, in big and little ways. "Have you noticed, dear, that you and

I have almost exactly the same purse?" she asks me, as we are putting away our things. I hadn't, but I tell her that I had noticed throughout the weekend that, in many ways, we have almost the same personality. She smiles in wry acknowledgment.

On a sudden hunch, I ask her, "Edith, when is your birthday?" She tells me it's October 24, which is also my birthday. We were both born on a Sunday on October 24—forty-five years apart. She is delighted at the synchronicity, and to my abashed gratification, she begins to refer to us fondly as "the twins." Over the years, as we come and go in our times together, here and there, a peculiar synchronicity remains. Though it changes from time to time, due to fashion and due to season, *we always have the same purse!*

She is home in California in her kitchen, briskly chopping up salad greens. She has been in her office all morning, corresponding with a student in Africa and talking to a dean at Yale on behalf of another student who needs an opportunity there. She runs out to the garden to cut some poke salad greens and calls out a friendly greeting to a neighbor walking his dog. She speaks to everyone as her respected equal and friend. After lunch, she presses an envelope full of poke salad seeds into my hand and tells me that they need sun. She returns to her office, her other garden, and continues tending to the well-being of people until sundown. She is a gardener, through and through. "If you know how plants grow, then you know how people grow too," she says.

I meet Edith at the airport in Minneapolis, and she emerges from the gate in a bright pink suit, her whole being sparkling with energy. I am nervous, eager to do all the right things, because I admire her so much. I am scattered and chattering, and unconsciously walking too quickly for the eighty-year-old woman beside me. She stops me with a strong grip on my arm and pivots me around to stand in front of her, holding me firmly by the shoulders to look me right in the eyes. Those eyes! So familiar to me, so ancient. "The most important thing of all, dear," she says, "is that we are together. Let's make sure we enjoy being with each other fully." My heart can hardly bear my good fortune. She slides her arm through mine, and we walk through the busy airport together, very slowly. At the baggage claim, she insists on lugging her own heavy suitcase along.

Edith was, for me, a mentor, a role model, a mother, and a friend. She truly embodied the grace of a *guru*, a spiritual master who helps you move from darkness into light. I longed for the kind of peace and power that flowed through Edith like a continuous waterfall of human glory. So I set myself on the same path that she had forged and followed: the persistent and unilateral practice of the universal law of Unconditional Love and Forgiveness. Two years after we met, I asked her to train me thoroughly in her life's work so I could teach it far and wide.

Edith recognized in me a kindred soul with a strong hunger to reach my potential and serve humanity in a meaningful way. I guess I also had some innate talent for teaching and counseling, so she agreed to my request and took me on as a personal student. She allowed me to follow her around like a lovesick puppy for a while, healing my sorry story and cultivating my leadership skills. I went to many of her workshops, at first as a desperate case, then as an assistant, and later as a teacher and an innovator with her method. Three times in ten years, I lived and worked with her at her home in California for ten days at a time, in what was certainly a rare opportunity for a personal growth intensive with an excellent psychotherapist. We did therapy sessions, I studied in her library, we cooked together, and we hung out with her husband, Paul. She held me lightly and firmly in her strong, aged hands, as a mother and as a teacher, while I grew up at an accelerated pace.

Eventually, I took my place at her side as her friend and peer in what had become *our* work. I brought her to team teach with me in a few places and showed off some of the creative innovations I had made in our workshop—some new tricks and exercises that help a group to bond quickly and increase the likelihood that every person in the room will be able to experience forgiveness. At the end of those last workshops we did together, Edith made it clear to me that she was pleased with how I was teaching her life's work and that she appreciated the way I allowed my creativity to expand and develop. "A real teacher hopes that their students will go beyond them," she told me, "and you are doing just that. Please keep doing our work, and allow yourself to do it even better than I ever did. I would like that."

At age eighty-five, Edith started slowing down, exhibiting memory problems and appearing to be a little too tired to command the room as she had when I first met her. She withdrew bit by bit from her stellar career and settled into retirement at last with Paul, her husband of almost seventy years. Edith and I kept in touch by letter and phone, and the last time I saw her was at her ninetieth birthday party. When the party was over, we sat together on her couch late at night, lingering over her cards and gifts, and Edith reminisced about each person and the eras of her life in which they had been closely connected. When Paul died a year and a half later, I received increasingly sad reports from Edith's daughter about her mother's deterioration. "The lady you knew isn't here anymore." Edith died peacefully at ninety-five, on October 26, 2004—right after our birthday.

For most of the years that Edith was my mentor, she was busy with her life in California, and I was busy in the laboratory of my life in Minnesota, mastering this forgiveness method. I enthusiastically practiced forgiveness of many things past: hurts large and small incurred as a child in an alcoholic family, losses of all kinds along the path of growing up, and all of the ridiculous indiscretions of my wild youth. Parallel to my healing and excavation of the past came the painful things in my present-time adult life: my two pregnancy losses, our failed family business, my husband's injury and ensuing chronic illness, my burdens as a solo breadwinner, worrisome events with my teen daughter, our home flood disaster, and my personal lacks and limitations as a small business owner. And parallel to *those* were world events requiring forgiveness for peace of mind as a citizen: disappointing elections, terrorist attacks, and climate change. Despite a little embarrassment about seeming like a religious zealot with the same answer for everything, I doggedly pursued the path of Unconditional Love and Forgiveness, personally and professionally. I was ready to roll with whatever life dished up, and as ever, it seemed to dish up plenty! I was committed to ending my own suffering by letting go of every disappointment, unrealistic expectation, grief, and attachment. I had the understanding and the tools to do so, and I knew from tried and true experience that if an expectation is causing me to suffer, I can work it out of my system—I have the power to release it! Dispel that suffering, *now*!

It was during this period of intense growth and experimentation that my mentor's model of Unconditional Love and Forgiveness morphed inside me into my method of Eight Steps to Freedom, as described and explained in this book. The book's title, *Unconditional Forgiveness*, is defined as a spiritual pathway that supports health, happiness, and freedom through the persistent and unilateral practice of the actions and attitudes of unconditional love and forgiveness. It is the decision to forgive everyone and everything, great and small, as a lifelong positive habit that increases both your personal well-being and peace in the global human community.

My all-out enthusiasm for the amazing relief of healing that forgiveness brings, which I've personally experienced, poured into my work as I taught others how to forgive as well. Beginning in 1990, I taught workshop after workshop in many venues and locations, always pleased with how friendly and adaptable my Eight Steps to Freedom are in a variety of different communities. I taught forgiveness in churches, universities, treatment centers, hospitals, and businesses. I taught it around the United States, the Republic of Ireland, and Germany. Always the audiences looked at me with the same human yearning, their eyes holding the same question: *Really? You mean I can get healing for this terrible ache in my heart? I can find a way to move beyond the pain of my divorce (or job loss, the death of my child, my friend's betrayal, my unexpected health dilemma, the cruelty of my alcoholic father)? Really?* Yes, really, I told them, and showed them how, as Edith had shown me. And I watched people heal swiftly and completely, every time.

The determination and resilience of the people who have passed through my workshops and my private counseling practice is a shining strand of continuous blessing in my life. I give thanks that my painful path led me to be a healer, teacher, and author. This book not only teaches my Eight Steps to Freedom, but also bears witness to the unlimited courage and durability of human beings. Despite the appalling number of sad and painful stories that my work has inevitably brought to my awareness, the power of the soulful healings that have taken place with each one has instilled in me a deep awe and respect for the glory and goodness of the average human being—we are amazing!

It seems universally desirable to have a practical way to end emotional suffering and heal the wounded human psyche, so I am going to share this process with you in a universal language. I want to see this book in the hands of all people—from any country, culture, or background—who are eager to learn how to forgive, because there is no country where the human heart is exempt from pain and disappointment. This book can be a helpful friend to open-minded people of all faiths as well as to nondenominational spiritual seekers—the lifelong students of personal growth who want to live their best lives. Therefore, I want to communicate the spiritual and psychological framework that surrounds my Eight Steps to Freedom method in such a way that it can teach everyone and alienate no one.

Although I speak to you from my own particular background, beliefs, and studies, and with my own words, I know that you will hear that I am speaking to you truthfully, from my twenty-five years of witnessing potent emotional healings: the spiritual ingredient is crucial for complete freedom from suffering. Therefore, I refer to "God" quite a bit in this book. In the same way I teach a workshop, I mix it up with the "God-language," use different terms, and draw upon various religious traditions and nonreligious resources. Please forgive me if I alternate between the use of a simple traditional word, God, and words like Universe, Divine Source or Force, Light, Creator, and so on. Let's give an appreciative nod in the direction of the Twelve-Step Program of Alcoholics Anonymous (AA), a program that has healed millions of people around the world over the last sixty years. With the simple phrase "God, as I understand Him" and the benevolently inoffensive terms "a Higher Power" or "a Power greater than ourselves," the founders of AA established a way to have people with different God concepts or none at all in the same room—in the same circle—helping each other to become free of a toxic, miserable state and to find healthy, meaningful lives. They tell their members, "Take what you need and leave the rest." My Eight Steps to Freedom method follows the same principal of AA: that there is a "Higher Power," however you choose to define it, and it is essential to the process of healing.

I will also speak the language of *energy* and refer to the subtle energy system, because it is the energy component of the Eight Steps to Freedom that makes this forgiveness method more genuinely renewing, physically, than many of the other more intellectual approaches that you can find out there. Energy is an essential thing, whether you are thinking about it from a spiritual or a scientific point of view. Through the ages, there have been a few different systems that attempted to identify how the flow of energy is organized within and around our physical bodies. Traditional Chinese medicine shows us the meridians, like rivers in the body, flowing with *qi*, and the Indian mystics show us the seven centers, or *chakras*, of the body, spinning the life force from the Universe into our subtle and physical bodies.

In this book, the depiction of the subtle energy system is a brief synthesis of general information that I have encountered in various studies over the years. The illustrations throughout feature only those elements that are the most useful for accomplishing forgiveness and being "centered" when you are in the presence of difficult people or situations. If you still have some hesitation, I encourage you to act in simple faith (because it won't hurt you) and see what happens. You will learn through your direct experiences of your own subtle energy system when you practice my Eight Steps to restore your peace and health.

I hope this book will be a good friend to you. I have written it as if you were sitting right here in the room with me, and I am leaning forward as I say, "Come on, I'll show you. You are going to feel better very soon." I've written it with the idea that it will help you move right through and out of something that is bothering you, and that *Unconditional Forgiveness* will be on your shelf for a long time, at the ready to help you deal with your next loss or disappointment. I've written it for you, as if we are compadres, mighty companions on the path to becoming whole and happy human beings—for indeed we are. Thank you for being willing to step through the door and onto the path that opens with the experience of forgiveness. Thank you, in advance, for the blessing of the new light that you will offer to the world as you shake off your fetters, breathe the fresh morning air, and lift your sights to the horizon.

1

Unconditional Forgiveness

The experience of forgiveness is profound and refreshing. When we do the gritty, methodical work that goes into healing and resolving an old hurt, we dissolve the stagnant weight of resentment inside us, and our bodies are flooded with new energy. Forgiveness mends our tattered personal boundaries, improves our health and relationships, and empowers us to move forward with hope and creativity. As we release the past, we also release ourselves into the richness of the present and the possibilities of the future. We find ourselves on new ground, ready to walk forward into our goals and dreams.

Nothing is unforgivable, and in this book, I want to encourage you to embrace the spirit of *Unconditional Forgiveness*. Forgiveness is a private process that we do for our own sakes, and there is no experience of hurt, loss, betrayal, or disappointment that is beyond our power to heal and resolve. When we forgive someone, we are saying that even though this experience of hurt (painful, difficult, unjust, abusive, and so on) has happened to us, we are going to completely release that pain and move forward without it. Even the most broken heart can be mended through forgiveness, and the steady practice of forgiveness throughout our lives will reframe for us the worst stories of our human journey. When we are wounded and suffering, an attitudinal choice lies right in front of us: will we feel and believe that we are victims of cruel fate, slogging through unrelenting and meaningless struggles? Or will we empower ourselves to take the opportunity to travel to higher ground, employing universal spiritual principles? In the hot laboratory of daily life, day by day and year by year—no matter how difficult it gets—each one of us has the power to transform our painful stories from those of a victim to those of a willing student of life. Like a master-in-training in a customized wisdom school, we can turn our wounds into wisdom as we complete each lesson of the graduate level course called Unconditional Forgiveness.

There is a spectrum of pain and healing in life that runs the gamut from the slight annoyance of being treated rudely by a clerk in a store to being let down by a good friend who forgot to come to your birthday party to the heartbreak of shattered marriage vows and all the way out to the horrible atrocities we read about in history books or see on the news. In each case, from the smallest to the worst offense, the organic process of healing the psyche is exactly the same—only the time it takes will vary from short to long.

Unconditional forgiveness is based on a model of health and well-being that is rooted in both modern transpersonal psychology and universal spiritual laws. The Eight Steps to Freedom is the method of unconditional forgiveness that reliably works to bring swift and permanent resolution of any painful emotional issue. These Eight Steps are effective because they arise out of a sound holistic understanding of how the psyche heals itself, as well as the timeless wisdom that tells us how to reestablish and maintain a sense of harmony with others and with the Universe. This is the same body of work that my teacher Dr. Edith Stauffer developed and taught as Unconditional Love and Forgiveness from 1970 to 1990, and that I inherited and refined from 1990 to the present day and have renamed the Eight Steps to Freedom. In the last forty years, this method of unconditional forgiveness has assisted thousands of people to release themselves from emotional pain and to change their lives for the better.

Unconditional forgiveness is a pathway toward enlightenment, if you will, which utilizes our difficult emotional human issues to teach us about our true nature as universal spiritual beings. In the necessary work of ending our painful suffering, we also transform our small, isolated sense of self by tapping into our connection with our Higher Self, and we give ourselves the gift of a solid and real relationship with this Divine Source. We discover that there is a great stream of love flowing to us from the heart of the Creator, and the blessings of life come steadily to us on that stream of love. In this way, our willingness and our discipline to forgive something that made us feel hurt and limited bring us through a doorway into a greater realm of trust, freedom, and love.

This book will thoroughly teach you the Eight Steps to Freedom, the process of forgiving any person or situation. And yes, I promise, we will also cover the important task of forgiving one's self. Let's review again the simple working definitions of unconditional love, forgiveness, and unconditional forgiveness:

Unconditional love is an attitude of seeing the good in any person or situation. It is also a universal spiritual energy, a Divine Force that restores you to wholeness and freely extends itself to all beings without limits, expectations, conditions, or demands. It is a way of being that blesses and encourages all to thrive.

Forgiveness is an attitude of being willing to let go of unrealistic expectations of self and others. It is also a tool, the process by which this release is accomplished. And it is the experience of the release itself—the dissolving of a stagnant and painful block inside you, followed by the sense of new open "space" and an influx of fresh new energy.

Unconditional forgiveness is the profound and transformative experience of completely releasing any expectation that is causing us to suffer—forgiving everyone and everything. It restores us to our natural state of wholeness and happiness that is independent of what others have done or are presently doing.

Reasons to Forgive Everyone and Everything

There are many reasons that people choose to learn how to effectively accomplish forgiveness. Here is a list of possible reasons:

- You are tired of suffering about something and need to move on.
- You want to reduce your stress and improve your health.
- You are on a spiritual path and want to reach your potential and live with purpose.
- You want to be a better Christian, Buddhist, Yogi, and so on, and *live* the forgiveness teachings of your chosen faith.
- You are in the Twelve-Step Recovery Program.
- You want to improve your relationship with a member of your family.

- You are a mental health professional and want a reliable tool to help your clients release the pain of the past.
- Joy!

You are tired of suffering and need to move on.

Life is difficult, and pain visits all of us on a regular basis. When we're children, we fall off our bicycles and scrape our knees or lose our favorite toys, and we howl with anguish that is barely addressed by the comforting things adults say. As we grow, we soon find out how cruel other children can be, and we struggle for respect for our individuality in our families. We see catastrophe and injustice on the news each evening, and as we venture outward into the world, we encounter the reality of the human shadow in certain incidents that harm our sense of safety, confidence, and our very self-worth. Even if we are blessed with thoughtful parents and fairly easy childhoods, it isn't long into young adulthood before we meet people who hurt us or situations that deeply disappoint us: the unappreciative boss, the charismatic lover with an addiction problem, the friend who turned away and won't come back.

If you are blessed with a naturally forgiving personality, you are lucky! You shrug off your bad experiences and keep moving forward happily and purposefully, despite the hurts of the past. But if you, like many people, are the type of person who closes down protectively and holds on to grudges, at some point, you should take some time to learn how to forgive so the accumulation of resentment won't negatively impact your health, success, and relationships. Sometimes you have to pause after a certain era of your life and do some housecleaning of the burdens and resentments you accumulated before you can move forward. Most of us have lists in the back of our minds of people and situations that caused us to close down our trust and our creative energy—a little or a lot. But you can work through such a finite list methodically when you finally turn your attention to the issue of forgiveness. For many of us, the biggest task is to forgive ourselves and come to terms with our limitations and perceived failures. It is a fine art, as well as a mark of spiritual maturity, to be able to accept yourself as you are and to peacefully live the life that is yours to live, day by day. After viewing the high-energy, glamour-driven modern world that is portrayed on television, you may find yourself subject to the delusion that your own life is falling short, somehow—that you are not beautiful or accomplished enough to merit your own admiration of who you are. The truth is that there is no part too small to play in this world. You are as necessary as the smallest ant and the greatest star. When you fully engage the life that is yours, accepting yourself as you are and your present situation exactly as it is, you may soon experience a beautiful paradox: your deep acceptance of the present will naturally empower you to create things as you wish they could be.

You want to reduce your stress and improve your health.

Healing stuck emotional issues, especially resentments, is a key to health and vitality. Holding on to negative emotions is destructive, no matter how "right" we think we are. If we do not completely process and release a hurt or resentment, we carry it around in our physical selves. We carry it in our energy fields, or in our muscles, joints, organs, and immune systems. We know this to be true, intuitively: if we are full of old issues it feels almost the same as being forty pounds overweight. We are tired. We get sick. We lose our joy. We live only half the lives we could be living.

"Your issues are in your tissues." Today this common sense truth is being tested and proven in scientific and medical research. In the last dozen years, thousands of new studies have emerged to explore the relationship between emotional toxicity and physical disease, as well as the relationship between the practice of forgiveness and the measurable reduction of physical stress (see Appendix E, "Current Research on Forgiveness and Health," on page 183).

People identified to be in toxic stress conditions who were taught to forgive:
- Lowered their blood pressure
- Improved their immune system response
- Reduced their anxiety and depression
- Improved the quality of their sleep
- Improved their self-esteem and sense of empowerment
- Reduced their stress
- Reduced their dysfunctional patterns of behavior
- Improved the quality of their personal and professional relationships
- Increased their energy levels
- Improved their sense of social integration and belonging
- Increased their peace of mind in daily life
- Increased their experience of peace in the dying process

People are starting to understand that the ability to forgive is, in fact, an important health habit and probably the next important public health issue. In the same way that we now understand that we should quit smoking, eat fruits and vegetables, drink water, and exercise, we are beginning to understand that hate and anger states are toxic to us, and that we need to learn how to deal with them. My own experience in twenty-five years of practicing and teaching a potent method of forgiveness has shown me time and again that a pleasant byproduct of emotional healing is the resolution of a physical health problem that was rooted in the emotional issue.

Here are a few times I've witnessed physical conditions resolving after forgiveness exercises:

- I have worked with three different people whose colon cancers went into remission after a short, intense bout of forgiveness work on historical resentments. All of these people were convinced that their cancers were caused by the huge pile of resentments that were "eating them up" inside, and that their forgiveness caused remission of the cancers.
- I had a student who cleared up a case of colitis that she had struggled with for sixteen years—the same amount of time that she was angry with her ex-husband! She had never made the connection between her issues with her ex and her colitis, but this persistent condition was 50 percent better the day after she finally forgave him, and the rest of it cleared up completely over the next six months.
- I reliably get a sinus infection after a week or so of being irritated at my husband about something. In her groundbreaking work *You Can Heal Your Life*, author Louise Hay explores the metaphysical connection between unconscious mental beliefs and physical disease. She claims that sinus infections start from "irritation with someone close to you in your environment." I think it must be true, because my sinuses start clearing and draining within hours of forgiving my husband. This little health phenomenon is a recurring reminder to me that I am only hurting myself by remaining irritated with my husband,

and that I want to live the way of unconditional love and for-giveness because it feels better. I may not like what he's doing, but I dislike sinus infections more. So, I forgive him because I want to be healthy more than I want to be right! And it's far nicer to see the big picture and feel love for him than it is to remain annoyed about the small stuff.

You are on a spiritual path and want to reach your potential and live with purpose.

What does the practice of forgiveness have to do with the fulfill-ment of your life's purpose? Quite a lot, actually. Forgiveness clears away the old blocks and outworn stories that obscure your innate gifts and obstruct your power. Real power is the unob-structed flow of Spirit through you and into the world. It is the expression of your most authentic way of being and living.

If the pipeline between your soul and your personality is blocked up with chunks of undigested old experiences, you do not have access to your creative energy, and you find you are unable to make things happen. If your true sight is foggy and out of focus because of old messages and archaic beliefs from your family system, you will not see and cannot be who you really are. Every single time you practice and experience forgiveness, you shed something false and invoke something true. When you take the broom and sweep the old garbage out of your heart, you make room for the scintillating light of your soul to slide into that empty space, bringing with it new clarity and new seeds of vision and purpose to plant and grow. As you open the channel between personality and soul, your creativity and intuition increases, encouraging and guiding you in large and small ways to fulfill your purpose.

So if you are lumbering along in the dark without a star to steer by, sometimes the surprising answer to the question, *What do I do now?* is the directive toward self-healing. Your soul whispers to you: *Forgive everything from the past that is burdening and confusing you. Clean your house. Then you can seek your purpose anew. What are you waiting for?*

Some of the most amazing people we meet are people with the worst personal stories. Their stories were their training grounds and the laboratories of understanding that became their greatest gifts to others. They discovered that once they digested and released the energy of sorrow and trauma, it was replaced by a large capacity for compassion, wisdom, and a passion to contribute to the well-being of others. The degree of personal greatness some people achieve is directly related to the amount of forgiveness they had to do. In this way, self-healing is intimately related to living a purposeful life.

You want to actively live the forgiveness teachings of your faith.

Unconditional love and forgiveness are spiritual practices based on universal laws that are part of the teachings of every great world religion. These spiritual practices, sincerely employed, bring new life and vibrancy to anyone's faith. To give only a few examples, forgiveness helps a Christian to love her enemy as well as her neighbor, and it opens the door "to the kingdom of Heaven within." It helps the Buddhist dissolve his emotional attachments to end his suffering and successfully be at peace with life's impermanence. A Yogi will come closer to his goal of uniting his personal self with Brahma, the Great Self, if his chakras are not all clogged up with stagnant energy and the blocks of old wounds that were part of this life's karma. A Jewish person can consciously choose to "clean house" at Yom Kippur if she knows how to use the Eight Steps to Freedom to clear up a relationship that got messy in the last year. Atonement happens.

I grew up in the Catholic church, where I heard about unconditional love and forgiveness many times, and I struggled with the concepts terribly. I knew that a good person is someone who loves her enemy and forgives everyone who hurts her, but it made no sense to me. I was taught that forgiveness is the *right* thing to do, because Jesus said to do it, but I never heard *why* it's good to forgive. No one ever told me that it would be beneficial to me personally—that I would feel so much better inside—and certainly no one ever showed me how to do it. Therefore, I felt guilty for being incapable of forgiveness and yet resentful about hearing so often that I ought to do it. Forgiveness felt like one more pressure on me, one more *should* that I carried around from my weighty religious training.

Now that I've learned about the miracle of forgiveness via a different avenue than the church and have experienced and witnessed the lightness that forgiveness brings, I think I understand why Jesus and other spiritual teachers made such a big point of it. The mandate from the masters to forgive is not just about being good citizens and sparing others the brunt of our hate. Rather, the message in all religions is that we are meant to be *free* and connected to the Divine Source—as Jesus put it, "to have life and to have it abundantly."

Every major world religion has a spiritual master at its origin, a great soul who was like a blazing lamp that kindled the fire of love and spiritual growth for people in their day, and for centuries afterward in the religions that grew from the master's inspiring example. Jesus, Muhammad, Buddha, and all the others walked this Earth, looked into the eyes of their people, and saw the terrible effects of resentments. They saw illness, lack of harmony, crippling shame, and poverty of spirit. From the Light within them, with great compassion, they each gave us the traditions of unconditional love and forgiveness, among other teachings. They may have used different words, but if we were to translate the essence of those teachings into modern day parlance, they would sound similar. It would be something like: *Come on, dear ones— lighten up! It doesn't have to be this hard. You're only hurting yourselves. Let go and live the universal law of loving one another. You'll feel better.*

You are in the Twelve-Step Recovery Program.

The work that goes into releasing resentments is a key factor for a successful program of recovery from drug or alcohol addiction. In fact, we can say that the process of forgiving yourself and others is a main component of the Twelve-Step Program. If you observe the Twelve Steps as a whole, you can see that there are three distinct "sections" in the plan. The first three steps are about starting a good relationship with a Higher Power, the middle steps have to do with forgiveness and cleaning up the past, and the later steps help us to deepen our spirituality and build new integrity into daily life. Step Twelve, the final step, which is also another beginning, takes us back into the world to serve others who are still in pain. The Twelve-Step Program offers us a stable place of growth: a group to witness our struggles and support our efforts with compassion and honesty, a new relationship with a Higher Power, and the thorough housecleaning of the debris left over from our destructive pasts.

Learning how to forgive, in real terms, seriously empowers one's recovery program. The work of self-healing is absolutely necessary in order to get us onto new ground in our lives and to prevent relapse. In fact, forgiveness is the best relapse prevention measure you can ever take. Once our bodies are free of the chemicals, and we are somewhat safe from the daily danger of using a substance, the real healing process begins naturally, in earnest, from a deeper level. Most alcoholics and addicts have unresolved grief and trauma issues buried away under layers of chemical use and compulsive or destructive behaviors. It's as if these big negative emotions have been frozen away like blocks of ice in the unconscious mind, and yet they take up so much room and drive many of our choices and behavior patterns. As these memories and feelings start to thaw out and make their way up to the surface of consciousness, we experience strange bursts of emotion, disturbing dreams, and problematic projections of our issues onto other people and situations in the present. Like Jacob Marley's ghost wailing, rattling his chains and locked boxes as he comes out of the dark cellar in *A Christmas Carol,* our hidden stories awaken and demand our attention at last. This is the point when we are in danger of relapse, because we are not familiar with how to heal our emotions instead of drugging them. But if we are serious about remaining sober, we must shine the light on those stories, face them full on, and call on powerful spiritual forces and effective therapeutic methods to redeem the darkness inside us.

We will be bolder in allowing this painful but liberating process to unfold if we already have some confidence in the power of healing and the power of forgiveness. Steps Four through Ten of the Twelve-Step Program are so much easier to accomplish if you have some vision of the feelings of lightness and freedom that are on the way because this is all about releasing things that are burdening you. If you make a commitment to forgiving yourself and all others, and you work your way methodically through your list, it may take a year or a number of years to accomplish, but you've got time. Forgive your parents, forgive your creepy uncle, your grade school teacher, your ex-wife, the people who turned you on to drugs and alcohol when you were very young—everyone. Forgive yourself for every small or large thing, as you're ready. Layer after layer, like the petals of a huge rose unfolding, each new healing reveals more of your authentic nature. This is the real stuff of purposeful living. And like the Twelve-Step Program, unconditional forgiveness through the Eight Steps to Freedom is a lifelong path, a new way of living that brings serenity and fulfillment.

You want to improve your relationship with a member of your family.

The people we love the most hurt us the most, even if they don't mean to. The people in our families with whom we feel a strong tribal bond can also be people who frustrate us with their inability to understand or share our important values on a day-to-day level. Our relationships with parents, children, siblings, and spouses can be very complex puzzles of love and frustration—we can't live with them and can't live without them. We often have long-held patterns and barely conscious formations of painful feelings formed by repetitive incidents related to our sense of worth and power that began when we were infants. Family members can trigger these patterns or painful feelings in the present, giving them a lot of power in our psyches.

For example, perhaps when you were a child your older brother hit you a lot when you were playing together and frequently called you "stupid." He did this because he was six, no one was watching, and someone at school had done this to him. You were four, and no one came to your aid at those times, so you logged some beliefs about your brother, yourself, and your relationship that still drive you in an embarrassing way, at times, in the present. He's nice now, you're both in your forties, and you have a PhD, yet you feel nervous and stupid around him. That's because there's a chunk of uninformed old energy inside your relationship that is like a stone in your shoe, keeping some tension there and making the relationship less rewarding than it could be.

That's a simple example, and most people have managed to navigate this sort of family dynamic successfully, polishing it off over a long period of time. But in many family relationships, the hurtful incident or series of incidents is more serious than that, and this creates a lifelong ache in the heart, or a pattern of reactivity that keeps stress alive in the family system. Forgiveness removes that stone from your shoe and takes that static out of family life. It gives you the power to be yourself with your family members in the present. You will have healthy new boundaries in place, and your attitude of unconditional love will smooth out the sharp edges and help you to enjoy these people. It is a very interesting phenomenon that as soon as one person does forgiveness work in a family system, there is a ripple effect that begins to change the dynamics between all the family members. Eventually, it spreads outward to the neighborhood, community, and global levels.

In the case of a more serious injury, betrayal, abandonment, or disruption between family members, the need for unconditional love and forgiveness is even more imperative. These emotional ruptures can keep you feeling sick and torn up inside and can consume your energy to the point of obsession and cause you to live your life too small. For example, you can't live day to night being disappointed in the character of your spouse and not also diminish yourself in a very real way. Resentment makes you harm your own character. You must forgive your family in order to re-establish your own self-respect again. It's an entirely separate issue whether you will remain married to your spouse, or allow a mean uncle to attend your Christmas party, or sue a relative who is cheating on the will. You might have to take actions that help you hold a boundary with a toxic person. Forgive the person completely first, and then make a decision regarding your healthy boundaries and right actions, and stick with it. Forgiveness is a cleansing experience that you do for yourself, and one of its many gifts is more mental clarity. Curiously, the private act of forgiveness makes your public actions flow with more integrity and harmony. Others in your family and community will see this and respect you.

Painful dramas aside, the people in our family are ours for a lifetime, to live with, to learn from, and to enjoy the best we can. All too often, we don't appreciate the goodness in these people that we see every day, and we take them for granted, like they're part of the scenery. It's a shame when we do not realize a family member's ordinary preciousness until he or she is gone. There is so much more enjoyment to be had in our relationships if we consciously try to see the good in people and take the responsibility to clear out the buildup of irritation that gathers inside us from a series of disappointed expectations.

I am so thankful that I managed to forgive and heal my relationship with my father, which was the most painful relationship I've ever had with anyone. He was a practicing alcoholic until I was fourteen. I was the oldest child, and in some ways I took the brunt of that family disease. I don't need to tell you the whole sorry tale, but in essence, I needed to forgive him for four big things: (1) he was not *present* for me as an individual because he was drinking and I was one of many children; (2) one time in a drunken blackout, he was very inappropriate with me; (3) he once failed to protect me from harm, and I got very hurt; and (4) after he got sober through Alcoholics Anonymous, he never made amends to me for any of his failings as a father during his drinking years. I worked in a treatment center for a long time and felt that I knew these amends were an important part of the Twelve-Step recovery process. *What kind of shoddy program are you working, anyway?* I fumed.

For twenty-five years, I hated my father, and my discomfort with him caused me to stay away from my family for a long time. My long-held negative feelings toward him alienated me from my siblings as well. None of them shared my history with him, and they could not understand my negativity toward the sweet, positive guy everyone knew and admired in the present time. When I did come home for a visit, the tension between my father and me was so thick you could cut it with a knife. "Why does Mary hate us?" my youngest sister asked once, after I left.

My father sighed and said to his plate of meat and potatoes, "She doesn't hate you, honey; it's me that she hates."

It took several distinct chunks of forgiveness work, which spanned a period of about five years, to completely heal this broken relationship. My wounds ran the gamut from intense rage about being mistreated while he was still drinking to extremely tender feelings of abandonment and the vague and desolate feeling that my father didn't like or respect me. I did all of this work privately, as my father had made it clear to me that he was unable to talk about my emotional issues directly. He couldn't do that with anyone but a few guys in AA. So I had to forgive him for that too.

Each portion of forgiveness that I completed brought new strength and detachment to me and my story. As I healed, a calm, clear flow of unconditional love began to grow between my father and me. Step by baby step, we awkwardly sought ways to connect with each other in sincere goodwill during the last five years of his life. We found our peace with each other in simple moments: watching a basketball game on television or taking an autumn walk around the neighborhood, our conversations and our silences growing increasingly natural. He managed to show me in shy, indirect ways that he did like and respect me, like the time when he grabbed my hand in his arthritic one and squeezed it as I walked by his chair while packing to go to the airport. He couldn't look at me, and he didn't say anything—just a quick, intense squeeze, his eyes still riveted on the ever-present newspaper. But what a warm flood of love enveloped me for a moment! By the time he died, our relationship was truly resolved, and my grief for him was soft and easy.

You are a mental health professional and want a reliable tool to help your clients release the pain of the past.

If you work as a professional in the field of mental health (psychologist, social worker, clergy, psychiatric nurse, marriage therapist, coach, and so on) you are probably a healer at heart, and you care about the alleviation of human suffering and the empowerment of others. There is a range of reasons why people get into this work, but I observe that most helping professionals have cultivated their careers as an outgrowth of walking the path of healing themselves. We are folks who long to grow into our full strength as individuals, and we want that for others. We hurt when we see another person hurting, and we wish to bring the right psychic medicine to that wounded psyche in front of us. Too often, we have been the consumers or providers of *talk therapy*—an approach that serves to release some stress and diminish some loneliness but usually falls short of providing real healing. It works only on the mental level and doesn't sink into the heart of an issue where it is lodged in our bodies and our energy. Talk alone does not provide the infusion of spiritual energy that is needed to powerfully dislodge and *change* a hurt from deep inside.

The word *psychology* means the study of the soul, yet most modern psychology has striven to keep the idea of the soul out of it, craving a scientific base for its validity. The life of the soul and the subject of forgiveness are both considered the territory of religion, but nothing could possibly be more important than these two concepts for the field of mental health. A powerful change is currently bubbling in this field: the growing awareness of the importance of including a client's spirituality in the therapeutic process, and the idea that complete emotional healing will come about with the true experience of forgiveness. These influences are bringing the possibility of real and lasting transformation for people seeking therapy.

Organically based personality disorders aside, any clients who really want to change *can* change, if they use an effective method of forgiveness on their wounds. Clients need to be capable of naming their wounds in terms of forgiveness, learning to use the method with your help, and connecting with a Higher Power for the spiritual energy necessary. Believe me—the hurts will heal. When a client trusts you enough, and indicates that she is ready to turn the corner on an old painful wound with a parent or someone else who has wounded her, it is time for you to offer the notion and the tool of forgiveness as the next step to freedom.

The best preparation for being a potent psychological healer using the tool of forgiveness is to practice real forgiveness extensively on your own issues. This will give you authority to speak about forgiveness with clients who need to do it but are struggling with willingness to forgive, or lacking confidence that they can succeed and feel better. *Authority* is a wonderful concept when understood from its root meaning: *one who knows*, because of his or her own study and experience. As you heal and integrate your own stories through forgiveness, you gather more and more spiritual light inside you, and the truth of this light speaks to your clients' souls directly. It invites them to trust, feel safe, and believe you when you communicate with them about the value of forgiveness. Every good therapist knows that healing has its own mysterious timing, and so much of it depends on the ability of the clients to believe in, and successfully navigate, a significant change that needs to be made.

Sometimes we have to do a lot of preparatory work with counseling clients to kindle their faith and their will for change. But once they possess the will and have been educated in the steps of forgiveness, and we know how to bring in the energy of their Higher Power in a way that is acceptable for them—it's time to go for it! How do we know when a client is ready to forgive? See Appendix C, "Suggestions for Psychotherapists," on page 173.

In my experience, there is little that is more rewarding or a greater honor than to be the facilitator of the experience of forgiveness for another person. In every forgiveness session, there is a very sacred, pivotal moment of change, when the fetters of the past dissolve and the client is released into the now, with all of its fresh possibilities. This special moment is a blessing to therapist and client alike. In the same way that every birth and every death is a sacred portal to Universal goodness for those present, the moment of forgiveness is a bonding moment for therapist and client. The client's first act of forgiveness is also a turning point in the therapy process. The forgiveness of lesser wounds, or smaller facets of a big wound, builds the stronger muscles needed to grant forgiveness at the gritty painful core of the worst stories. The refreshing experience of forgiveness inspires one to do more forgiveness and to take this healing work to its natural completion.

You are ready for a more joyful life!

Is there any good reason to cling to guilt, shame, pain, and suffering? All of these things dampen our spirits and inhibit the bright expression of the joy that dwells in our essence. It is high time we rid ourselves of the grim vestiges of soberness and rigidity left over from prior eras—eras that were characterized by harsh struggle or a paradigm that preached shame and was driven by fear. Why do we still hold back sometimes from being fully happy? Birds chirp, squirrels chase each other, otters swim and dive, dogs wag their tails, cats purr, monkeys joke, wolves cuddle, eagles soar the heights, and babies laugh about their toes. Joy is the bright Force of Creation that throbs through all of its creatures in different ways. Joy is God's song, and it sings the flowers awake in springtime, calling out with conviction that there is no ultimate death, no winter that lasts. Joy is the Earth turning her face toward the sun once again, and the frozen hard ground yielding and softening, like our hearts when they are given hope that they might heal and be happy after all. Joy coaxes the sap to rise, the trees to extend their branches into space, and the blossoms to burst slowly forth with color and fragrance to share their particular songs with whoever will come by. We are surrounded by a chorus of the sublime and the beautiful, and we need to let ourselves sing gaily in that grand chorus. Joy! Why not? It looks good on you.

Tackling the Problems about Forgiveness

Hopefully, some of your problems about forgiveness are starting to relax as you get your mind around what forgiveness really is. I know you will continue to warm up to your enthusiasm for forgiveness as a way of life if you also clearly understand what forgiveness is *not*.

Forgiveness is not:
- **Forgetting.** You don't have to "forgive and forget." Honestly, does that ever really happen? It's much better to forgive and remember, instead. It's wise to remember what really happened, and how people really behaved in a particular situation. Some people are not to be trusted in certain ways, and you already learned that from your unhappy experience with them. You must remember who people are, not who you'd like them to be. As Maya Angelou put it, "When people show you who they are, believe them, the first time."
- **Excusing.** The people who have hurt you have possibly done something that is very wrong, and wrong is wrong—that's all there is to it. When you forgive someone, you don't excuse the person's wrong actions; you merely detach yourself from your involvement in that person's actions and drop your burden of pain about the situation.
- **Saying it's OK if it's not.** Some things will never be OK according to you, because they offend your value system or because a person has broken a clear agreement he or she made with you. That is not OK, but you can hold your opinion about that loosely by releasing your emotional hostility from that opinion.
- **Being a doormat, open to further abuse.** With real forgiveness, you learn to set healthy boundaries and to say *No!* to things that are not right for you, and stick with that. If you can say that *No!*

in a spirit of neutral goodwill instead of hate, you will be able to move into better and healthier relationships in the future. You will be empowered by the act of forgiveness, and your boundaries will become stronger.

- **Reconciling.** You don't have to hang out with someone, stay married to him or her, talk things out, make amends and apologies, or wait for amends and apologies if that isn't appropriate for your situation. It's nice when that can happen, but often it doesn't. Sometimes the person you need to make peace with is completely inaccessible or has died. You can still make peace with people who are not around. Forgiveness is a private action that you do for yourself.

- **Giving up.** Sometimes people are afraid that it is weak to forgive, that they are giving up a battle they must continue to fight. But when we forgive, we are not giving up our value systems, our points of view about an injustice, or our right to dislike someone. We are giving up a rigid attachment to thinking that things could have or should have gone differently. We are giving up the pain from our disappointed expectations. We are *giving up the hope for a better past*, therefore giving ourselves the gift of a richer present.

- **Justice.** Sometimes we can experience a measure of restorative justice in a situation—a lawsuit settlement, an apology, or a vindication of ourselves in an unfair situation. But we have to let go of our addiction to worldly justice and trust in a higher court of justice. Whether we believe in the Golden Rule, the Law of Karma, or Judgment Day, our spiritual intuition tells us that all people are subject to the laws of the Universe, and good and wrong actions will eventually be rewarded or corrected by that just, impersonal Law. Ultimately, nobody gets away with anything! If we can let go of our demands to get justice the way we see it here and now, we will be at peace sooner.

Why We Resist Forgiving

There are many reasons we may be reluctant to forgive someone or something. Let's explore a few common ones.

I need to protect myself from getting hurt again.

No one wants to be a doormat, subjected to the serial wrong behavior of another person. So we keep our anger alive as a means of protection, a wall around our hearts that will prevent us from trusting someone and then being sorely disappointed again in the future. Unfortunately, that wall keeps *everything* out, even good things like joy, abundance, and the love of others. Even worse, it keeps out Nature's vitality and stops the healthy flow of communication between our personal self and our Higher Self, or soul. Doubly unfortunate is the fact that the wall itself is ineffective, because we are actually *more* vulnerable to similar offenses until our wounds are fully healed. It is counterintuitive for our egos to forgive someone, but if we do it anyway, we will discover that life is better without the wall.

But don't I have a right to be angry? Especially when what the other person did was wrong and unjust?

You absolutely have the right to be angry at an unjust person or situation. Anger is a natural response to injustice, and good, healthy anger floods us with adrenaline, courage, and will. It pushes us to step forward and set things right. It is good to speak and act upon healthy anger in a responsible way when we feel righteous indignation. Sometimes we have to draw the line with someone and use some power and heat—whether it's taking him or her to court for cheating us, fighting for a fair deal in a child custody case, or firmly telling a person to *get out, now!* But anger is meant to be a temporary state, not a permanent one. It is the doorway to the house of wholeness and power; it is not the house itself. You can't live in a doorway; you have to walk through it into a new attitude of peaceful resolve and choose what you will and will not allow from people in your life.

I don't want to forgive the person because I know that I am right.

Maybe you are in the right. Maybe you are standing on the higher moral ground in this situation, and the other person is clearly wrong. You feel that someone ought to hold the person accountable, and so you are doing your best to bear witness to this injustice—afraid that if you don't, no one will, and that person will get away with it. Something inside you doesn't want an injustice to be allowed to stand, unchallenged and unrectified. So you remain attached to being right, but that attachment causes you to suffer. *You* are the one who is obsessed, and you are the one who is losing sleep over someone else's actions—therefore, *you* are the one who will have stress-related health problems. Meanwhile, the villain in this story might be peacefully unconcerned about his wrongdoing and blissfully unaware of your rage—and he is sleeping just fine at night!

There are laws of justice in society, and it's nice when things unfold fairly, according to your sensibilities of what is fair. But you don't have control over that. At times, you need to forgive a grossly unfair situation so that you can sleep at night, and turn that person and situation over to a higher judge and law than you can see. You need to take yourself off the job of being the judge of another person and focus instead on your own integrity and your own life's purpose. Let the other person sort it all out with a Higher Power at some point. You need to move on. As Marianne Williamson has put it, "Do you want to be right, or do you want to be happy?"

What if the offense is ongoing? How do I forgive him if he's going to do that same annoying thing again tomorrow?

Sometimes we must interact with people who behave in a hurtful or offensive way every day. You may not be in a position right now to leave your spouse, your teenager, or your boss. But if you forgive people like this for the load of things that are piled up inside you from the past, you will be less reactive in the present and can let go of your stressful response to them more swiftly each new time the same thing happens. Eventually, you will attain a degree of detachment and even a sense of humor about someone's annoying behaviors. This does not mean that we are excused from good communication with our family members or coworkers. We must lobby for what we think is right and healthy, if we are able. Very often, after we have forgiven someone, our voices are empowered and our communication abilities are heightened, because we are able to approach the person with goodwill and no judgments. This enables him or her to better hear what we are saying. Ultimately, if we are involved with someone who is dysfunctional, we must decide for ourselves where the boundary is and make the painful choice to allow the relationship to continue, or not. If we stay, we stay knowing it is our choice to do so. If we leave, we will do ourselves a huge favor if we leave in a state of acceptance and forgiveness.

If I forgive him do I have to tell him about it?
Do I have to enter the relationship again?

There is a difference between *forgiveness*, which is a private experience that you do to heal yourself, and *reconciliation*, in which two people rebuild a broken relationship, usually with the help of a third party. There may be a time during reconciliation in which you grant forgiveness in service to clearing the past offense and rebuilding trust and new agreements for the future. It is possible, however, to completely forgive yourself and the other without ever seeing or speaking to the person again. Just be clear about what you really want.

I don't want to feel the pain from terrible times in my childhood.

Nobody wants to bring up old pain. Nobody wants to go to the dentist to have a cracked tooth pulled, either, but at some point, we tire of our chronic pain and take steps to resolve it, even if we have to face more intense pain for a short time while the dentist pulls the tooth. Forgiveness is like that. The truth is, you already have this terrible pain going on inside you, even if it is muffled by a few layers of denial or addiction. It is warping your life and dimming your happiness every single day, and it is causing you to stay small and live small. We tend to stay numb and keep childhood's pain buried and swaddled up because (1) we do not have the resources around us to deal with it effectively, and (2) we are afraid to take the lid off the emotional equivalent of Pandora's box. We fear that if we tap into our deep sorrow we will sink into a sea of depression and be incapacitated at work, or if we feel and express our honest rage we will break something, blow up a building, or do physical damage to a family member. Those things won't happen if you decide to work through your issue with my Eight Steps method and if you have a good support person in attendance while you do it. It's actually difficult to hold on to sadness and rage for very long, once we grant ourselves the full freedom to express it in a safe space. Our emotions come out completely in Step Two, and then we move along to the next steps until the process is complete and there is no more pain. Aah, relief. The wonders of modern emotional dentistry are impressive.

I don't want to let go of my grief— this loss is so important that I can't rush it.

Grief is an important, sacred process that slowly allows us to release the powerful energetic bond that we have with another person. It does take its time, and we need to allow ourselves to be with grief for a while. Grief comes in chunks and waves, releasing its memories and feelings in portions at a time, so our psyches can process the loss without becoming completely overwhelmed and incapacitated. I have found that the forgiveness process is supportive to the grieving process, allowing me to fully enter and "complete" each wave of grief as it comes along. It is a way of sifting our experiences and claiming the spiritual gifts of the lost one into our awareness, like jewels. Grief and forgiveness are both a process of *incorporation*, meaning *to bring into the body* the wisdom available from this relationship with a person who has had a big impact on us.

The person I need to forgive is dead. I've lost my chance to work this out.

You can forgive anyone who is causing you distress in your heart and mind, whether the person is dead or alive, near to you or far away. Forgiveness is an inside job, an internal, private experience that you can do for yourself at any point in time. It does not require the physical presence of someone, nor does it require verbal reconciliation. You are always in the driver's seat when it comes to achieving inner peace. If you want to reconcile with someone after she is gone, you can send her unconditional love and a wish for goodwill between you—wherever she is—and she will receive it. Her body may be gone, but her soul is alive in God's Universe, because the soul is energy, and energy is indestructible. You haven't lost your chance.

I mostly want to forgive and feel better, but there's a part of me that is refusing to do it. I'm fighting with myself about doing this.

We all have more than one voice inside us, and a number of "parts" or sub-selves that seem to have minds and lives of their own. In transpersonal psychology, we refer to these uncooperative parts of us as "subpersonalities," and sometimes we have to work with our resistant subpersonalities before we are clear to move ahead and make a change (see Appendix B, "Notes on Psychosynthesis and Transpersonal Psychology," page 169).

I'm afraid to let go of this old story and move forward. It's been a part of me for so long that I don't know who I'll be without it.

The experience of letting go of a big, long-held hurt is so life-changing that you might fear it, because most of us fear the unknown. This deep and permanent healing of your formative wound is a death of sorts for the distressed ego, which has long identified with the wound and adapted its daily behaviors around it. But it is also the rebirth of your authentic soulful self into the present day, and the freedom to start anew. What *do* you want to do with a fresh start? Are you afraid of freedom and happiness? Many people cling to an issue for years because it is a familiar form of suffering. They unconsciously prefer that familiar pain to the fear of moving forward into unfamiliar territory, even if that new territory is love and happiness. Do you identify with your role in the old story: victim, hero, brave fighter, forgotten child? How about growing up at last and learning to identify with your resourceful and elegant soul, one day at a time?

What if this issue comes back again? What if it doesn't work?

Real forgiveness is a transformative process, not an adaptive one. It is a permanent healing because the old issue inside you is completely dissolved by the steps in the process. Think of a solid wooden log in your fireplace. When you subject it to the transforming properties of fire, the log is burnt to ashes, and ashes it remains. You don't burn a log to ash and wake up the next day to find that it has come back again. It's still ashes the next day, and the next. It has been changed. And so will you be.

Anyone Can Learn How to Forgive

Most of us were taught to read and write, wear clean clothes, and take good care of our teeth, and we were clearly instructed in how to drive an automobile—but we were not taught how to handle our emotions and losses in a healthy and whole way. If we had a religious upbringing, perhaps we understood that we *should* forgive, but no one ever showed us *how* to do it. In fact, forgiveness is a skill that can be taught with the same kind of clarity that we expect in a driver's education class. I wish it was part of junior high or high school curriculum, in the kind of health classes that discuss sex education and drug addiction prevention, because the effective healing of emotional pain is also a universal health issue. It isn't hard to forgive—you just need to know how.

Try to imagine this with me. It's an elective class, and in this peaceful classroom, a small group of young people meets with the teacher in a circle. The class meets twice a week for a whole semester. For the first few meetings, the teacher establishes ground rules for respect and safety in the group, and the students participate in simple trust-building exercises so that they can set aside their perceived differences. Bit by bit, the teacher introduces the curriculum for wholeness, and the model of soul/personality psychology gives each teenager there some new ground to stand on, with a lifeline to soulful serenity as they navigate the turbulent waters of adolescence. The instructor teaches the steps of forgiving another and encourages each person to share a current painful issue with this budding community: *My parents are fighting.... My boyfriend is breaking up with me because he likes someone else better.... My friend has been hurt in a car accident....*

With the skilled facilitator, one by one, they find relief for the issues they chose to work on. When the teacher leads the whole group through the self-forgiveness process at the end of the course, the embarrassing mistakes of teenage life are softened and released. Each person there experiences the powerful way that losses and mistakes can be lifted to a new level of learning: a personal body of valuable life insights and wisdom that will build on itself in coming years. Like a tree, steadily growing bigger each year, ring upon ring of wood creating strength, these young people get the hang of being healthy much sooner than you and I did, and they grow spiritually strong and mature with startling rapidity because they are fed and bolstered by the authentic life of the soul. The group as a whole becomes a lamp of hope that illumines the path forward and starts a buzz in the school community. Shy but eager, more people sign up each semester, and the healing influence of unconditional love and forgiveness ripples steadily outward into the school and into the world.

Far-fetched? I don't think so. We live in transformational times, and big changes in society are rapidly unfolding because they are so needed. As a species, we are learning how to face the pain of human existence and how to wisely integrate our difficult experiences as a normal part of living our lives. This awakening of millions of individuals is going to influence our ability as a collective to make the shifts in societies and in our global awareness that we have been yearning for.

Let's take an overview of my Eight Steps to Freedom now and begin to get acquainted with them. Try to see from the beginning that this is an organic process, a natural flow of sorting out an emotional problem with a person or situation through all the parts of your being. These steps address the issue first in the personal self, or what I call *personality*, which is your basic, everyday human self and its different components: body, emotions, and mind. Your personality has a name, a history, genetic influences, formative events, talents and limitations, and so on—your basic identity. After addressing the issue in the parts of the personality, you move to the level of the Higher Self, or *soul*, the unlimited and eternal part of your consciousness. The soul is a source of light and healing energy that is connected to a greater Divine Source in the Universe. In forgiving another person with my Eight Steps, you bring healing into yourself as well as send goodwill to the other person, and you complete the journey of forgiving by choosing to see the good in the person now and into the future.

Eight Steps to Freedom

- *Prepare for a Change in Your Life.*
- Step One: State Your Will to Make a Change.
- Step Two: Express Your Feelings Exactly as They Are inside You.
- Step Three: Release Expectations from Your Mind, One by One.
- Step Four: Restore Your Boundaries.
- Step Five: Open up to the Universe to Get Your Needs Met in a Different Way.
- Step Six: Receive Spirit's Healing Energy into Your Personality.
- Step Seven: Send Unconditional Love to the Other Person and Release Him or Her.
- Step Eight: See the Good in the Person or Situation.
- *Integrate Your Change and Start Living in a New Way.*

In chapter 3, I will go into each of these steps in depth, explaining how they work and exactly how to apply them confidently to one of your emotional issues in the near future. You will see that the act of forgiveness is no longer a mystery, but something that you can learn—like driving—and use for the rest of your life.

2

Forgiveness from the
Mundane to the Catastrophic

Time heals all, it is said, and that is basically true, if one is open
to healing. Fortunately for all of us, there is a Divine Force in the
Universe that wants everyone in Creation to thrive. When any
creature, great or small, is wounded, a healing process immediately begins to mend us. This healing Force is what closes skin
over a cut on your finger within a few days, and it runs your
immune system so you will return to normal in a week or two
when you get a severe head cold. This invisible Force fills in the
gashes made in the surface of the Earth through industry or dis-
asters and slowly adorns her with miraculous new life after the
lumbering is over or the volcano has spent its fury. This quiet
Force of healing is what eventually tempers and adjusts the irasci-
bility in a dysfunctional family system; across space, over time, it
nudges individuals forward to finally seek understanding and to
once again extend the handshake of kinship. We can say that this
Force of healing is one of the laws of the Universe, the Law of
Restoration. Perhaps the Law of Restoration is related to the Law
of Karma, that great eternal balance-maker that teaches and

restores our souls and the groups of souls with which we are involved.

Humanity's literature and cultural storytelling around the world are full of the theme of healing. We believe in it more than we believe in despair. Even the worst stories—betrayal, murder, torture, war, and genocide—eventually yield to the gentle and powerful trend toward healing and wholeness. It might take a lifetime for an individual to heal, and it might take several generations for a family who fled genocide to fully heal. But healing eventually does come. It comes more swiftly if you are open and seek it, and if you use your will to attain it. When you consciously cultivate your awareness and understanding of healing, you will be amazed at your ability to open up to life again, despite the difficult stories your soul has asked you to live through. *Forgiving the unforgivable* is one of the most beautiful challenges a human being can undertake, and it teaches you that resilience and resurrection are the true strengths of human nature. If you consciously choose to add in some proactive emotional intelligence and some potent tools to accelerate the healing process, you can really impress and inspire yourself! *Wow! I actually got through that ... I am happy and at peace after all....*

You can see a demonstration of the healing process when you observe how healthy children behave when they hurt themselves. If a child falls off his bike and scrapes his knee, the healing process kicks in right away. First, he begins crying with abandon (no hold - ing back, no apologies, no trying to get himself to stop). Then, he runs for comfort and attention, *and he shows someone his wound.* He does not hide it or say, "No big deal," "I'm OK," or "It is what it is." The wound *is* a big deal, and he wants another person to see it and know exactly how hurt and upset he is. He cries loudly and points to the bloody scrape, and through his tears, he tells the story of what happened. "*Waaaaahhh!* I was riding over to Joey's house on my bike ... and I didn't see the bump in the side-walk and I couldn't keep my bike straight ... and I fell all the way off, and—and—look! *Waaaaaaaaaaaaaahhh!* Look at my knee!" The child shows the wound, tells the story, cries and cries, and receives attention.

In this scenario, the adult involved is also healthy and knows how to deal with emotions, so she listens patiently, murmurs soothing things, and does not try to talk the child out of his feelings. Many of us were told instead, *Stop crying, it's not so bad, you're too big to carry on like that. Shh! Don't cry—here's a lollipop.* (So *that's* how the sugar addiction got started!) When we were growing up, our well-meaning adults tried to stop our pain by getting us to stop expressing our feelings. In fact, what they did without realizing it was to *stop the healing process*. We learned to be embarrassed, ashamed, or numb when we were hurt and had feelings about it, even later in life. We became adults who hide our pain or medicate ourselves with something because we don't have a good way to deal with our emotions. We believe we are being weak or a bother to others when we show our pain.

Now, let's go back to our lucky, healthy child with his emotionally literate adult. The child is still crying, and the adult is holding him lightly, giving him compassionate attention and murmuring soothing words. After the child has let a lot of tears out and looks like he is ready to move along, the adult offers him a bandage and holds him some more, silently transmitting the energy of comfort and assurance from her heart to the child, who soaks it in. Together, they stay in that healing space until the child shifts his focus to something else entirely and is ready to go play again. For a while, the "owie" still hurts through its bandage, and he winces and tells someone else about it a few more times. The scrape develops a scab while new, pink skin grows under it. When the scab falls off, the spot is pink for a little while but no longer hurts to the touch, and eventually it blends in and the whole incident is "forgotten." More accurately, the memory drops down into the child's unconscious mind and becomes part of a bank of learning that subtly informs him the rest of his days about the need to avoid bumps when he is on a bicycle. But there will be no scar, and he will not fear riding his bike.

We can learn a lot from children when it comes to healing emotional losses and the cuts and scrapes of the heart. Like a child with a scraped knee, we need to discharge our emotions by crying or expressing anger; we need to show our hurts to compassionate people—a therapist, friend, or support group—and receive their undivided attention. We may feel the need to tell the story a number of times. Each time we tell it, we integrate some more insights that were hidden in the story. We might need a simple action that symbolizes "first aid" at the beginning of a loss, like the presence of a friend who runs over to spend some time with us, picking up Chinese food on the way. Or we might like a ceremony of closure as we reach the conclusion of our healing journeys (for example, reading a letter aloud at someone's graveside). You will see that a few components of this simple healing process are part of the Eight Steps to Freedom.

The Spectrum of Pain and Healing

When it comes to pain in human existence, no one is excused. Pain is part of life's curriculum, and there is a spectrum of painful experiences that runs the gamut from the mundane to the atrocious. We are usually managing pain at some level or another, even if we are fairly happy. And all of us like to tell or hear stories about the pain and healing of others, whether they are known to us or whether they are wounded folks being viewed en masse on the evening news. Here's a visual notion of the spectrum of pain. Obviously, this is not a conclusive list, but you will get the idea.

Irritation
- Traffic jams and parking tickets
- Bugs that bite
- A hard day with children
- Unfairness in household chores
- Pesky responsibilities you wish you didn't have

Annoyance
- A neighbor with a bad attitude
- Bad service in a restaurant
- Personality quirks and odd "tics" in people you live or work with
- Sibling rivalry

Mild frustration
- A child refuses to learn something you think is vital.
- Your spouse is always late for family events.
- Your friend complains about the same thing all the time but won't make a change.
- Daily life circumstances deny you the time you need for yourself.

Deep frustration
- You live with an uncomfortable and limiting chronic illness (yours or another person's).
- Your spouse doesn't understand you in some important ways.
- Your boss is inconsistent, unsupportive, and demanding.

Disappointment
- No one remembered your birthday.
- You didn't get the job you wanted.
- You worked very hard to win at something but didn't make the finals.
- Your dad got sick on your wedding day and couldn't participate.

Mild emotional upset/hurt feelings
- Your spouse doesn't notice you as a lover anymore.
- Your spouse takes you for granted.
- You have a fight with a friend, based on a misunderstanding.

Big emotional upset
- Your spouse makes a significant mistake with finances.
- A teenager in your family attempts suicide.
- Someone you love is destroying themselves with an addiction.
- You discover that a family member has been lying to you.

Mild trauma
- A car accident injures you and causes you pain and lost time.
- Someone attacks and robs you on the street.
- You have an unusually difficult experience in childbirth.
- Your house floods and there's a lot of damage.

Serious trauma
- You lose your home in a natural disaster.
- You become paralyzed after a fall.
- Your parent or your spouse beats you.

Wounded heart
- Your parents neglected you emotionally.

- Someone you really like broke up with you.
- You were abandoned by your parents at a key stage in your development.
- You are excommunicated by your church.

Broken heart

- Your marriage hits the rocks and can't be reconciled.
- Your parents get divorced and you don't see one of them anymore.
- You lose a child in an untimely death.

Major betrayal

- Your partner and your best friend have an affair.
- Your board of directors turns against you and fires you from the company you founded.
- Someone in your family spends a lot of money on your credit cards without permission.

Shattering event

- You are raped or sexually abused.
- Your family is broken up by war and scattered to various locations abroad.
- You witness one parent murdering the other.

An atrocity

- Your town is attacked and destroyed; your family is killed or missing.
- You are captured and tortured by an enemy.
- A terrorist attack kills and maims many innocent people.
- A malfunctioning nuclear reactor poisons a region of the Earth.

Pain Is Unavoidable; Suffering Is Optional

We cannot avoid pain, but we can choose to deal with pain in such a way that it does not become chronic suffering. Suffering is caused by our attachment to expectations of how people or situations should be, when our egos insist that it is not right that we are in these painful situations. When we are in a state of suffering, we cannot think of anything but the pain. When we are handling pain in a healthy and mature way, we face our losses and disappointments *open-heartedly*, exactly as they are. We grieve honestly, and then we release our expectations, one by one. In doing this, we release ourselves into the present time, as it is, and we discover that there is still plenty of love and goodness to enjoy.

I want to restate this now, because it is important: *From the smallest irritation to the most severe atrocity, the process of healing is exactly the same.* It simply takes a shorter or longer time to complete the healing process depending on the amount of pain that is stuck in the emotional body. It may take me two minutes to release the expectation that caused me to feel annoyed with my child, or two months to get over being dumped by someone I was dating, or two years to mourn the death of a close friend. Nevertheless, in each case mentioned here, I am ultimately letting go of an expectation of how I thought things should have gone or should still be today. Here follow two stories from the lighter end of the spectrum of pain and healing, to demonstrate the process of releasing expectations in action.

Two Stories from the Lighter End of the Spectrum

Even in a life that is blessed with good relationships and secure finances, we can find ourselves dealing with the mild frustration that attends daily life and its unexpected chores and obligations. Let's talk about a "normal" day with young children. Studies show that, contrary to popular myth, most people's reported level of happiness drops significantly when their children are born; happiness goes up again when children are "leaving the nest." Researchers surmise that this is due to the fact that the demands of raising children, day by day, force us to put our own individual needs and pleasures to the side for long periods of time, creating a low-grade experience of loss and frustration. We adore our kids and wouldn't send them back even if that was an option, but truth be told, raising children is extremely demanding and frustrating. Good parenting requires an athletic practice of unconditional love and forgiveness, because we need to release our expectations of our children and ourselves a dozen times a day.

An Extremely Ordinary Day

I wake up dead tired. There's nothing wrong, really. It's just a week with a lot of life packed into it, and I'm not sleeping well lately. I'm fifty-three, and my body is so hot every night that I'm tossing and turning all night long to cool off and get comfortable. So this morning finds me brain-dead and exhausted. But I know how to plod forward like a faithful and dumb old workhorse— I've had to do it so many times—so I make it through the morning tasks of helping my sixth grader, Vivi, get out the door with a good breakfast in her and a good lunch with her. When my neighbor Anne arrives to drive Vivi to school, she hands me a bag of *warm*, homemade blueberry muffins in a brown bag. I cuddle the bag to my chest gratefully as I wave them off. It seems like a sign, and I read it to mean that this tired morning of mine will soon be redeemed, and that I can have a charmed day after all, if I intend to. Before me lies an unscheduled hour to settle down in my cozy chair and pay myself a little attention by meditating, reading, and eating a blueberry muffin before I have to meet my scheduled obligations. Aah. There's nothing better than an empty hour.

The phone rings, and I am dismayed to find myself talking to a woman who has showed up at a campus across town for one of my trainings that was originally scheduled for today but was canceled a few weeks ago. I guess she never got the email saying that it was canceled, and she is more than disappointed. She sounds very distressed. "But—but—I've got to see you and get some help today! This issue with my sister is driving me crazy, and she's arriving for a visit tomorrow! Can't you please squeeze me in?" I can hear her need. I can feel the familiar nudge of Spirit at my back: *Go on, help her. Today's the day for it.* And darn it, I have just enough time to meet her at my office and give her some time before the other things I have to do. Long habit kicks in, and I mentally release my expectation of starting my day out in a mellow fashion. Instead I run out the door with bad hair and drive across town at top speed to meet her at my office. *But my time for myself?* I whine to Spirit as I drive; there is no answer. I meet the woman, and we have a good session.

So starts the day and night entitled: "Everyone and Everything Needs my Attention, *Right Now!*" It's early spring, and my business, like the Earth, has started sprouting. Back at my home office, there is a sudden influx of calls to return from clients and students. I receive an email from a television producer in Iowa, who proposes to do a special about my forgiveness workshop. This is gratifying, but now I need to help her write a proposal, *today*, because everything in the world of television is *Right Now*. This kind of business activity is what I long for in slow times, but

I'm tired today and I'd rather not talk to anyone. But I must, so I do. I still have three or four time-sensitive details left hanging as I dash out the door to pick up Vivi at school. As I jump into my car and it revs to life, I pause to close my eyes for ten seconds and take a few slow breaths, releasing my expectation that I will finish those things today. It's not going to happen.

I'm picking Vivi up half an hour early today because she and I have been pressed into babysitting service for my oldest daughter, Tara, who is twenty-four and a single mother of twin girls. Mia and River are charming, high-spirited three-year-olds, and we have a growing bond. I have to say that, like most adults, I feel outnumbered in the company of even one three-year-old, and having two of them from Friday afternoon until late Saturday morning is an athletic commitment of patience and endurance. But Tara has a strenuous schedule and is stretched for childcare, and I am the Nani (wise and brave), and Aunt Vivi is a marvelous help. Therefore, a few weekends a month, I square my shoulders and answer, *Of course I will!* when Tara asks me to do the long bout of childcare that goes with her Friday night waitress gig.

Thankfully, Vivi and I get home half an hour before the twins are due to arrive, and I head straight to my chair for that bit of meditation I was looking forward to. The phone rings, and Tara is there, breathlessly explaining, "I'm out in front with them, sorry we're early, we were out shopping, I'm running late getting ready for work, they're all set, can you just come outside and get them right now?"

I think to myself, *Darn*. I say out loud, "Sure honey, I'll be right there." I swiftly release my expectation that I can catch my breath, and I march resolutely outside to meet my duty. Mia and River are already standing on the sidewalk holding their respective toy animals, Sheep-y and Baby Elephant. They smile at me knowingly, as though they, too, cannot *believe* how cute they are in their new spring skirts and spanking-clean white sneakers with pink trim. They are both talking at once:

"Nani, we're sleeping over at your house, can we go for a walk to the swings?"

"Grandpa will be a scary monster and we will scream!"

"Can we watch a movie?"

"I'm hungry!"

"I have to go pee-pee!"

"Mia pushed me over and I cried!"

"Can I have the Winnie the Pooh bowl?"

"Watch me run!"

"Watch me run too!" And, like precision athletes, they take off down the sidewalk at full speed, trajectories at a forty-five degree angle. Within ten feet of the great running effort, they smash into each other with a resounding thud of heads colliding and bounce backward onto their bottoms simultaneously, howling. Tara throws the overnight bag onto the boulevard and waves trustingly at Vivi and me as she peels out of there—she is already talking on her cell phone. Vivi and I trot over to pick up our respective twin and bring them inside.

It's really OK being with the two of them if there are two of you, and if you keep an impeccable awareness of timing regarding food, drink, and the potty, as well as the balance between activity and quiet time, and structure versus go-with-the-flow. You can't try to get any work done, and you can't cook anything requiring attention to seasoning. You can't talk on the phone for more than three minutes. If you follow these rules faithfully, there are no meltdowns, nothing gets wrecked, there are no potty accidents, and no one gets hurt.

Everything is going fine until my friend Caroline calls. She tearfully tells me that a friend of hers has just committed suicide. Oh, no. Of course I must stay on the phone with Caroline and say comforting things to her as she sniffles mournfully and tells the story. I minister to her for ten minutes, as it is impossible to limit such a conversation to the allowable three minutes. She has no idea how tense I am, or what might become of my house soon, because the three minute rule is broken! This isn't good—the twins are out of sight, and Vivi has disappeared. I don't have the heart to tell Caroline that I must get off the phone, because of course this is a terrible thing she is dealing with. She is in mild anguish as she tells me that somehow this could have been prevented—there must have been *something* that someone could have done . . . . Now there are some alarming noises coming intermittently from around the corner, and these noises are growing louder as I continue to murmur gentle things. My whole body twitches with anxiety. Suddenly, Mia appears, eyes shining. She holds a toy wrench over her head triumphantly and shouts, "Nani, we're wrecking things so we can fix them!" River skids into view next to her, flailing a plastic hammer, grinning in affirmation.

They both trot out of sight again, and I say abruptly to Caroline, "Oh my God, hon, I'm so sorry about all of this—it's really not your fault. I will pray for her soul—I've gotta go!" and hang up the phone with a slam.

Vivi reappears, and we work in tandem to contain the chaos and put things back in place. D'oh! There is one big wet splotch on the carpeting in the middle of the living room and a trail of telltale drops heading to the stairs. Later, I find the wet, twisted underpants that one of the twins left on the floor near the toilet, mission not accomplished. Meanwhile, Mia has wandered onto the front porch, where the dog sleeps, and has discovered by stepping in it that the dog has had a poop accident. She trails disconsolately through the living room, distressed that her pretty pink and white sneakers have poop on them. She's not as distressed as I am when I see the trail of brown spots on the carpeting behind her. But long habit kicks in once again, and I try to "see the good" and thank the Gods that my fastidious husband is out of town and can't see these terrible things happening to his house. It would drive him to some sort of brink, but if I just keep moving and use the right household cleaners, he'll never notice. So I remain brave and positive as I whip the shoe off Mia's foot and run down to the basement to wash it. The twins follow me down there, talking nonstop over each other in amazing non sequiturs while I hover over the utility sink and scrape dog poop out of all those tiny little flower patterns punched into the rubber bottom of the shoe. Soon it is a pretty shoe again.

Bedtime is highly successful, with the twins tipping over unconscious halfway through *Skunks! Go to Bed!* (I have mastered the art of mesmeric reading.) I leave my little skunks sleeping in their portable beds set up in my basement office, with the baby monitor on so I can hear them from my room on the second floor. It's not the most convenient arrangement, but it's the best one we can come up with in our little house. I am yearningly thinking about the novel awaiting me in my bedroom, but Vivi wants me to cuddle with her and watch serial reruns of her favorite detective show, so I do. When I can't stay awake one more minute, I kiss her goodnight and enter a night of murky nonsleep.

Under the best of conditions, I am a light and dodgy sleeper, but tonight would put the best sleepers to the test. As I drift into the warm vicinity of personal renewal at 1 AM, the baby monitor in my room crackles with loud static and then erupts with a loud yell: "I WANT MY MAMA! *WAAAAAAAHHH!*" I leap into the air as if scalded and race down two flights of stairs to find both twins sound asleep. I stand there staring down at them, my heart pounding. I can't even tell which one of them had cried out. I climb back up two flights of stairs and lie down again, reviewing all my self-soothing methods as I try to fall back asleep. It takes a little time and a lot of discipline because there is also a loud drunken conversation going on outside in the distance. This is not uncommon in the city on weekend nights. I tune out the drunks, do progressive relaxation, and soon, I am almost asleep again.

At 3 AM, the low static of the baby monitor crackles to life and rips open into another sudden explosion: *"WAAAAHHH!"* I leap into the air and race downstairs, this time making rhythmic bangs because my groggy body weaves and slams back and forth against the walls of the stairwell as I run forward. When I get there, my heart is pounding and my shoulders are bruised, and once again I find two unconscious girls peacefully sleeping. As I slog slowly back up two flights of stairs, I am too tired to find the attitudes of unconditional love and forgiveness. I can't do it, and I lose all sense of positive ground to stand on. So I hiss things into the dark like, *This gig sucks! I'm never doing this again! She can just find someone else for Friday night! I'm too old for this shit!*

As I lay back down in my sweaty, rumpled bed, the drunks outside rev themselves up to call-the-police level. A landslide of negativity starts tumbling through my psyche, and I begin to think murderous thoughts—thoughts about genetically annihilating anyone with the DNA codes for alcoholism and a big mouth.

I get up and look out the window to see that the police are already out there, and so is an ambulance, and various people are being loaded into various vehicles. I hate them so much I'm not even worried about what they did to each other. While I'm at it, I just go for it with hating everybody and everything. The landslide inside me becomes an avalanche. I hate my husband, who isn't even here. *Why the hell do we still live in this shithole? Where the hell is he now, anyway? Sleeping in a cabin in the woods while I'm taking care of everyone and everything!*

Don't go there. Don't go there. Don't go there. Some part of me desperately tries to throw me a rope as I hover, rocking on the edge of the chasm called A Very Bad Attitude. I find a tiny spark of will, and with one final, resolute huff, I expel my hate and exasperation and grab the rope. At 5 AM, with two hours of night left before me to rest, I forgive, forgive, forgive this stuff of an ordinary day. I release all my wishes and expectations: that the twins sleep quietly through the night, that they are home at Tara's with her nonexistent husband instead of me, that my husband is home tonight, that I live somewhere peaceful, that I will get any sleep at all tonight, that tomorrow I will be less tired than I was today. . . .

As the sky grows pink with dawn's light and I finish my wrestle with forgiveness at the end of an extremely ordinary day, sheer exhaustion brings me to the edge of sleep at last. But just before I drift off, I hear another sound from the baby monitor. It's a quiet snuffling and grunting sound, almost like a little animal. It softly says *eh-eh-eh*, repetitively, in what sounds like helpless little animal distress. It is not one of my twins. The sound continues, pathetically, but now it is punctuated with the sound of a gentle woman's voice, murmuring soothing things. She sounds kind and centered. She is helping that little animal thing to calm down. *What on earth?* I wonder blearily. After a few minutes, I hear the unmistakable noises of a baby nursing, and a mother speaking low words of utter love and steady reassurance. Understanding slowly dawns in my aching head: my baby monitor is picking up sounds from another baby monitor nearby. I can hear the private pre-dawn moments of my neighbor Mary and her week-old baby, Ruby, two houses away from me. I feel slightly guilty. I'm a helpless voyeur to a moment of profound intimacy I haven't been invited into. But it can't be helped, and it's nice to listen to them. In two hours, there will be three-year-olds and an eleven-year-old, and my husband will return from the cabin, and I will like him again. I will be busy and tired, and my work will remain unfinished for another day. I smile a little as I fall asleep, because I am glad to know that, two doors away, hidden from view in the noisy inner city, a tender new life is starting out in the rosy glow of unconditional love. I believe that God is a Mother who looks after us all, and when I wake up, I will eat a blueberry muffin.

The Neighbor from Hell

Most of us have one of these at some point in our lives: The Neighbor from Hell. This is someone who seems custom-designed to annoy you, whose personality seems to defy all that you hold dear and decent. The daily presence of this person consistently inspires you to ask the questions, "How can anyone be so awful? And why do I have to deal with them?" Interacting with this neighbor is the best classroom in which to practice and master the art of unconditional forgiveness.

"OK," I told myself, "let's try this again. . . . Hello, Angie! How are you today?"

As usual, my next-door neighbor Angie muttered something under her breath, grasped her grocery bags a degree tighter, and stomped into her house like an angry troll. It might have been "hello" that she muttered. Or it might have been "go to hell"; I wasn't quite sure. Her pudgy face always wore the same scrunched-up, bitter expression, no matter what she was saying. I was going on my fifth year now of unsuccessful attempts at a friendly interaction with this woman. Why did I still bother?

Well, for one thing, our houses literally butt up against each other, crammed like hapless siblings side by side on our crowded inner-city block. In the summer, with the windows open, I can hear her (horrid, gravelly, screechy) voice, yelling at her kids like a fairy tale hag, even when she's in a relatively good mood. Because we live in the inner city, it is imperative that neighbors know each other and look out for each other. Everyone knows that. And why shouldn't she be friendly at this point? My husband had kindly mentored several of her wild sons, gently inserting some missing male nurturing whenever he could, and I was sure he had already altered their trajectory toward the state prison. We helped her get a grant and pick paint for the outside of her house, and I gave her my beloved old blue couch when we got new furniture. I piled on the goodwill with my friendly greetings to her for five years, and I still got no more than a reluctant squawk out of her each time.

The only time Angie ever wants to share with me in a neighborly way is when she is dying to report some bad news or say something very negative about what is currently going on around us in the neighborhood. *Then* she can talk, I tell you. With passion and in detail, with multiple paragraphs, she will stand on her decrepit front stoop, make eye contact with my left shoulder, and generously deliver her worldview to me: *Life, and everything and everyone in it, sucks.* For a long time, I tried to meet her rare outpourings with a response in the genre of *positive thinking/problem solving/we're in this together/let's look at it this way/how can I help you?* Nothing I said ever made a dent in her outlook or her relationship to me. Yet I kept trying.

Why, you ask, *can't you see when you shouldn't bother trying to talk to someone?* I'm afraid I can't. It's my upbringing. I was raised in an impossibly friendly Irish American family, in a Chicago neighborhood that was full of second-generation Irish Americans. It was hard-wired into me from an early age to be welcoming to everyone and to establish a "cousin-ly" relationship with one and all as swiftly as possible. In my neighborhood on the South Side of Chicago, we really had *neighbors,* lots of them, and the rare unsociable person was a pathetic anomaly in the sea of unreasonably hospitable people all around us.

When I moved to Minnesota I discovered that most people here are also extraordinarily pleasant to each other, a social phenomenon that has been given the cultural moniker "Minnesota Nice." We are nice because we implicitly realize that we must watch out for each other's survival and sanity each winter. Winter here is six months long, and it requires neighborly acts like shoveling our common sidewalks, pushing each other's cars out of drifts, and stopping immediately to help any stranger who is pulled over on the side of the road, so they don't freeze to death. Even more important than any of these courtesies is the expectation that we will wave in an encouraging way at each other on particularly nasty days and that we will notify each other if we need to move our cars when the streets are being plowed after a snowstorm. Otherwise the city of Minneapolis will tow the car away at great expense to the owner, and it takes a while to get it back.

So you can see that Angie's unfriendliness toward me was doubly baffling, and I stubbornly refused to accept it. I expect my next-door neighbor to be friendly to me, and I'm sure you agree that it's the right way to be. I continued to be unrelentingly friendly to Angie, and over and over I repressed the mild hurt feelings that always arose inside me because of her lack of reciprocation. But the moment of truth finally arrived one cold winter day—the day I finally realized that Angie would never be a good neighbor to me. That was the day she didn't even *try* to stop the tow truck from taking my car away from the front of my house.

Normally, if you don't realize that the snowplow is coming and you have to move your car *right now*, a neighbor will pelt up to your doorstep, ring the bell and shout, "For God's sake, move your car! They're coming!" If they're a *really* good neighbor they might stand by your car bumper in the cold morning air, bouncing up and down to keep warm, smiling and pleading with the parking enforcement officer and the tow truck driver, pointing to you running out of your house in your pajamas and bare feet, jingling your car keys.

Angie didn't do any of that for me. In fact, she apparently watched the parking attendant come and leave a ticket on my windshield, and she watched the tow truck come and hoist my helpless car onto its flatbed, all the while she was right there, shoveling snow. She didn't ask them to hold on a minute, and she didn't ring my bell. I came outside and saw my manacled car swinging around the corner and out of sight. Instantly, my day was changed for the worse, because I knew I was going to spend $150 and several frustrating hours before I had my car back again from the city impound lot.

"Oh my God!" I said. "The snow plowing! I forgot! Angie, didn't you see them coming?"

"Yeah," she replied, not looking at me.

"And you didn't come tell me to move my car?"

"It's not my problem," she said, still looking away.

I felt my fingers curl involuntarily into a fist. A murderous flush filled my head, and my limbs started shaking with adrenaline. I suddenly wanted to grasp her by the hair and bang her thick head down on the sidewalk, over and over and over again. Five years' worth of piled up resentments exploded in my brain, and this time I wasn't going to hold it back. "*Angie!* That is so, so, so ... *not nice!*" (Boy, I really know how to let someone have it.)

I tossed my head and huffed back into my house, swiftly securing myself behind the locked door of my basement study. And then I really did let her have it. I imagined that she was right there with me, and I uncorked a torrent of rage that involved pretending to smash her ugly face on the floor numerous times and shouting, "You hideous old bitch! I *hate* you!" over and over. I sobbed, I punched, and I wailed for my lost car and the $150 that the wretch could have saved me with the simplest act of kindness. After a while, I began to make my way through the rest of the steps of forgiveness. The essence of that task was releasing my long-held hope that she would one day warm up to me and be a decent neighbor. The final healing of this cranky little story occurred as I sent her unconditional love and good - will, *exactly as she is.*

After an hour of facing the truth in my study, I was physically spent, but my mind possessed a crystalline clarity about my relationship to Angie, and I made a few decisions about it. Fifteen years later, this clarity and those decisions still serve me well, every single day. This is what I've learned, and what I now completely accept: *Angie is not, and never will be, a friendly person—nor will she ever be a good neighbor to me.* It's merely a fact of life, like the sky is up and my dog has a tail. I no longer feel resentment, irritation, rejection, or annoyance about this fact of life. And this is how I behave: I do not say hello to her, and I do not seek her involvement in any neighborly concerns. I pay extra attention to the snow plowing days because I have one less neighbor watching my back. If I am walking out of my house in the morning at the same time as Angie to my left, and my other neighbor, Nancy, on my right, I cheerily shout, "Good morning, Nancy," and say nothing to Angie.

Am I punishing Angie with that behavior? Absolutely not. I feel quite neutral inside when I see her, and it no longer hurts me in the least that she doesn't say hello to me, even though I am only a few feet away from her. I walk serenely and silently past her, feeling as little obligation toward her as I do to the tree over my head or the lamppost near my car. She has become a neutral feature in my environment, sans meaning to me. And mostly, I don't say hello to her anymore because it finally dawned on me that she probably finds *me* annoying when I do so—like some overtalkative parrot squawking positive psychobabble at her when she's just doing her best to be left the hell alone!

My teacher Edith once taught me that a humble person helps other people get what they need and meet their goals—no matter what they are—if it's practical to do so. If it is Angie's goal to be left the hell alone by everyone outside of her immediate family, then I can help her out with that. It won't kill me to completely ignore my next-door neighbor even if it goes against my preferred values. I guess that's how you love an antisocial person. I suppose I would still gallop over there to help rescue her from a fire or a criminal if it was called for. But now, out of respect for her apparent commitment to no interaction, I don't invade her space anymore.

The one exception to our silent coexistence happened a few years back, and I treasure it. I was in the middle of making waffles for my daughter one morning and I urgently needed an egg. My neighbor Nancy wasn't home. I was feeling particularly intrepid and un-hurtable that morning, so I knocked on Angie's door. Without preamble or explanation, I fearlessly asked her if I could have an egg. Wordless, she left me standing on the stoop for a moment as she disappeared into her cavernous house. She came out onto her step, holding the egg slightly behind her back, and looked up at the sky, not at me. "Sure is a crappy day," she growled. "Yeah!" I belted out enthusiastically. "It totally sucks!" With a ghost of a smile, she handed me the egg and went back inside.

3

Eight Steps to Freedom

Let's get started now with understanding the nuts and bolts of this healing program and learning the *why* and the *how* of each one of the Eight Steps to Freedom. This is an orderly, step-by-step method that is based on the natural flow of the healing process as it occurs in most people over time. In her forty-five years of experience working as a psychotherapist, my teacher Dr. Edith Stauffer observed thousands of people make their way across the landscape of healing the psyche, and she noticed that there are certain tasks to be accomplished and certain universal milestones along the way that signify that a real change is occurring. She assembled these tasks and stages into the Unconditional Love and Forgiveness method, which I later renamed the Eight Steps to Freedom.

This method is something that you can choose to do proactively instead of waiting for the fullness of time to bring healing. Edith fondly looked upon the Unconditional Love and Forgiveness method as her "recipe" for forgiveness, and she shared it far and wide for twenty-five years. "When you have a good recipe for something that everyone wants to know how to cook, like chili or brownies—a simple recipe that always turns out well—you are eager to share it with everyone who is open to it."

The reason that this "recipe" for forgiveness is reliable and transformative is that it is holistic and complete, assisting you to swiftly and permanently release the painful effects of a wound, no matter how large or small, and no matter how long this issue has been held inside you. It works the issue out of your system by addressing the wound on all levels of your being—physical, emotional, mental, energetic, and spiritual—and sets you on new ground in your relationship with life. Our forgiveness method is not merely an intellectual or moral exercise, and you will not have to force yourself to remember your resolution to forgive someone, again and again. Once you've done it, it's done. You will have changed deeply inside yourself, and the issue will be truly resolved.

Eight Steps to Freedom
- *Prepare for a Change in Your Life.*
- Step One: State Your Will to Make a Change.
- Step Two: Express Your Feelings Exactly as They Are inside You.
- Step Three: Release Expectations from Your Mind, One by One.
- Step Four: Restore Your Boundaries.
- Step Five: Open up to the Universe to Get Your Needs Met in a Different Way.
- Step Six: Receive Spirit's Healing Energy into Your Personality.
- Step Seven: Send Unconditional Love to the Other Person and Release Him or Her.
- Step Eight: See the Good in the Person or Situation.
- *Integrate Your Change and Start Living in a New Way.*

Prepare for a Change in Your Life

A person's attitude toward forgiveness as a life habit is intricately connected with their attitude about change, in general. We need to know how to forgive, because life is always changing and when we practice effective forgiveness, we change ourselves too.

Embrace change

Are you ready for a change? Do you like change, or fear it? When you seek the experience of unconditional love and forgiveness toward a person or situation you have felt "stuck" about, you are taking a step toward a change in your life that will manifest in a number of large and small ways.

When it's time for a change, it's time for a change. It's hard to say why people hold on to a problem for a long, long time and then realize that they want to be done with it. More than once, I have had someone call me up to do a forgiveness session or sign up for a forgiveness workshop, after carrying my card or flyer around in her purse for ten years! One spring morning people wake up, I guess, and think: *I'm tired of hating my ex. I'll get over it now. Where's that card?* Later, after they've spent a short time working this thing out of their systems and they feel light as a feather, they wonder: *Why didn't I do this sooner?* It is a perennial fact of life that most people are afraid of change.

I once saw Edith attempting to work with a woman in her forgiveness workshop who was not yet ready for a change. The woman was in her mid-fifties, and she had carried her bad story around with her since she was twenty. She was aware that this old issue was affecting her health and her marriage, but she was hesitant—holding back from letting it go. She resisted Edith's attempts to help her through Step One (State Your Will to Make a Change). So finally, Edith asked her, "How much longer would you like to carry this terrible burden in your heart?" The room was silent and expectant while the woman closed her eyes and searched for her answer. We all wished she would let herself feel better, *now*. Why wouldn't she? Wasn't thirty-five years long enough to be angry about something? After a long pause, she opened her eyes and said calmly, "Until October." (This was in May.) Edith nodded, baffled but accepting, and the woman took her seat again as Edith asked for another volunteer.

Fear holds us back from making changes that are good for us, and it is the masterful human being who takes charge of this tendency and learns to consistently move through fear and stagnation to embrace change and reach the frontiers of happiness. If you decide to make forgiveness a way of life and a regular habit, you will take a huge step toward being a soul-illumined person who is living in harmony with life. Life is not only full of change; life *is* change. A masterful person is someone who chooses to move with life's movement, trusting herself and trusting God. When she is afraid, she reminds herself to keep breathing and open up instead of closing down. She encourages herself to take the next step. How do you encourage yourself? How do you prepare for the life change that healing your big wound will bring to you?

Set the stage for a permanent healing of your issue

Seek inspiration. Think about your heroes and how bright and productive they are—how they don't hold themselves back with stupid old resentments. Remind yourself that you want to be like them, worthy of your own admiration, and that you can dare to be great too. Remember your postponed dreams and encourage yourself to move forward, in small steps, toward a better life.

Analyze why you have been holding on to this resentment, and ask yourself how much longer you want this burden. Review the potential benefits to you now if you let go of it.

State a firm intention, out loud, to yourself and another person: "I will move on now and forgive that person, once and for all." Give yourself a deadline for taking action.

Educate yourself about the steps to forgive another, and get ready to apply them to this person and this situation. If you wish, use a notebook to record specific painful incidents, and try to discern the expectations that went along with them.

Arrange the time and space to do the forgiveness session. Allow two hours, in a private space where you will not be overheard or interrupted. Do this when you'll have some time off afterward to digest your experience.

Get a good support person to be with you while you forgive, if it is a big hurt. (Smaller ones you can do on your own.) This might be a trusted friend, a Twelve-Step sponsor, your minister, or your therapist. It should be someone who is accepting and not judgmental, comfortable with emotions, and connected to a spiritual Source—someone you can pray with and cry with. Ask your support person to familiarize himself or herself with the Eight Steps, a little, before your meeting.

Set up the room you will work in: sit next to your support person and place a chair out in front of you, at least four feet away. The chair can be empty, or have a photo or an object representing the offender sitting in it. Have tissues handy. If you have a lot of anger, have props ready to help you get it out. (Examples: a big cushion and a tennis racket, a bat and punching bag, a cardboard box you can punch and break, a broken household item you can smash up with a hammer, paper to tear into little pieces.)

Gather your intention for complete release and healing, and pray for support. When the room is ready, sit quietly for a moment with your support person, so both of you can gather your intention to go all the way through this healing process to the other side. Imagine Spirit's presence in the room with you, and say a prayer out loud asking Spirit to help you get to the heart of the matter and release yourself from it, *today*.

Visualize Spirit's Light like a canopy of loving protection stretched across the upper space of the room you are in, and clearly imagine the person you are forgiving sitting in the chair across from you. Then go on to Step One.

Step One: State Your Will to Make a Change

Your will is "the chooser" inside you. It is the invisible spiritual muscle that you use any time you make a life change for the better. The will is the mechanism by which you choose your goals and attitudes and hold them in place until you achieve success. Your will makes you stand up, step forward, take risks, exercise self-discipline, act with courage, make a plan, and execute that plan to completion.

In Step One, your will gives you:
- Motivation to make a major change in attitude and seek a fresh start
- Discipline to make the time and place to sit down and do a difficult thing
- Determination to start the process and get all the way through it
- Courage and honesty to face your painful emotions
- Firmness with which to reestablish your personal boundary
- Ability to surrender, to let go of expectations you strongly desire to have
- Power to send light and goodwill to someone you have been hating
- Strength to choose to "see the good" in the person from now on

How to do Step One:
1. Place an empty chair out in front of you, and clearly visualize the person you are forgiving sitting in it. Use a photo or symbol of the person if you wish.

2. Imagine your will like a sturdy flame within you, giving you courage.

3. Say out loud, "I will forgive you now, because ..." and state the reason(s) that you need to forgive the person and why you are willing to do it. (Examples: "you hurt me so badly," "I've carried this pain long enough," "I am ready to let go of this trauma," "I need to move on," "I am tired of thinking about this," "I want to be done with you," "I want to use

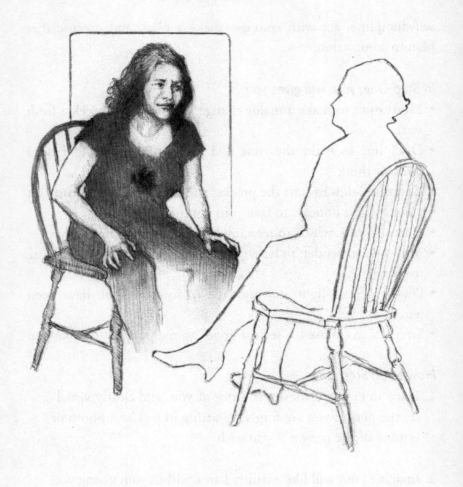

my energy for my goals and dreams," or "I want to improve our marriage and be in love with you again.")

4. State your will to forgive the person, out loud, with firmness and conviction.

5. Go on to Step Two.

Step Two: Express Your Feelings Exactly as They Are inside You

Your emotions have their own truths, different from a mental truth or a spiritual truth. Your emotional truths need to be spoken plainly, perhaps accompanied by the physical discharge of crying or venting anger. For example, in dealing with an irresponsible ex-husband who is an active alcoholic, a woman's mind might try to be detached and positive as it says, *Well, he is a very sick person, and I know that he can't really help what he's doing at this time. I'm just grateful that I'm separated from him now.* Her mind believes these things, yet she still has a lot of hurt inside. Her feelings want to hotly declare, *That stupid son of a bitch! If he ever shows up drunk when he comes to see our son again, I will kill him!* That is her emotional truth, which is on a different circuit than her mind. While her mind might wish to maintain detachment toward her diseased ex, she will have a restless struggle with her mind until she gets those angry emotions out. The emotional truth wants its due. In her emotional self, this woman wants to shout, cry, punch something, stamp her foot, thump her finger into her ex's chest and tell him he is worthless, and fantasize other violent or vengeful things. The emotional energy is whirling around and around inside her chest, throat, and belly, and she needs to let it out. Her backlog of unexpressed rage from the past will hurt her body with stress every time this guy messes up in the present or future.

When you release anger, you need to understand that you are not hurting anyone if you vent it in this therapeutic space. Your mean words and feelings spoken in a forgiveness session are not hurting anyone or creating more violence in the world. You are merely using those words to move the stuck energy of old anger out of your body. Your expression of anger may be big and hot:

you may pace, shout, swear, accuse, punch and kick soft objects, or break something you've decided ahead of time is OK to break. Or your expression of anger may be cool and stern: you may just lean forward in your chair, speak vehemently, and break a little sweat. What's important is that while you are speaking, you are aware of moving this anger *out* of your body, *out* of your space, once and for all. Aim it with all your might at that empty chair.

If you are healing sadness, you need to speak from your heart and belly, softening those blocked, hard areas with breath and tears, and peeling down and down into the layers of feelings until you find the difficult, tender things that have been hiding inside your sweet, disappointed heart. Rejection, abandonment, betrayal, feeling unwanted and unloved and unlovable ... dare to feel those difficult feelings directly, and say them out loud, honestly. Then they will move out of you, and you will open up again and move on. It may seem to you that if you really admitted how terribly sad and hurt you feel, it would crush you, but the reality is that there is only a finite amount of pain inside, and you can empty that bucket. When you cry deeply and hard, or when you are feeling despair, it seems as though there will be no end to it. As you sink deeper into the waters of emotion, your toes will touch the bottom of it eventually, and you start shifting out of it sooner than you'd imagined you could. It is actually pretty difficult to cry for longer than twenty minutes. Twenty minutes of weeping feels like an eternity of sadness when you are in the middle of it, but in fact it is such a short amount of time in your life—think of your daily commute to work! The reward you will gain in the feeling of ease and release inside is huge! Afterward, you will wonder why you didn't face this little old pot of pain and empty it out sooner than you did.

I once worked with a man named Joe who was bowed with grief, literally, for the son he had lost sixteen years earlier. The little boy had died suddenly at age six, in a freak household accident that his father had been unable to prevent, even though he was right there. His last word was "Daddy—!" Joe was wracked with shock, horror, sorrow, and guilt, and despite a number of bouts of therapy and participation in grief and loss groups, Joe could not move on. A very tall man, Joe walked with his head bowed and his eyes cast down a lot of the time, obviously oppressed by the pall of sadness that weighed him down.

When I met Joe, he expressed his desire to finally let go and move on, but he didn't know how to do it. He had cried rivers of tears over the years, but his grief didn't seem to lighten up at all. He and his therapists were frustrated and bewildered. As Joe and I explored his issue in a circle of very compassionate people, we found that he had some feelings he had never yet expressed, because he was afraid they were wrong and unfair feelings to have. Emotions are neither fair nor rational, and truth be told, Joe felt angry at his son. He was angry that his son had left him and ended their precious father-son relationship. He was angry to be deprived of the rewarding experiences he had expected to enjoy as a father: watching his boy grow bigger, attending his games and graduations, teaching him to fish and to drive, and having long talks together as father and son. Since his son was a baby, Joe had imagined him growing up to be a good and handsome man who would get married, become a father one day, and share the joy of long-term family life with Joe.

He had to overcome some resistance to go there, but with my encouragement, Joe imagined the soul of his son (no longer a little boy) sitting in the chair, and he expressed his anger and his "selfish" disappointment about all of these things. It did feel kind of "wrong" to give his child a hard time about dying accidentally, but I reminded him that these are only emotions. Once Joe got over his trepidation about saying such things, the honest feelings just rolled out of him for twenty minutes, and he visibly lightened up as he went along. After he released his many expectations of the future, and we made our way to the end of the steps, something wonderful happened. As he sent his love out to the soul of the boy somewhere in the Universe, Joe's posture unbent and his head lifted, as long tears of peace and love slid down his face. "I can feel him!" he whispered. "I can feel my son's spirit, right here with me. He is smiling and laughing and giving me so much love.... He says he's been right here all along, and he's been waiting for me to finally notice.... I was too sad and mad to feel his spirit until now."

As you can imagine, there wasn't a dry eye in the room. As we closed our circle that day, we found that we were all looking up at Joe now, who was standing at his full height for the first time. His head was level, and his eyes were looking out, not down. He said, "I feel like I am looking at the horizon for the first time in sixteen years, since my son died. I had forgotten there was a horizon." Over the next two days, any time I noticed Joe walking around, talking to others, or getting food in the cafeteria, I couldn't help but notice how tall he was. I couldn't believe the peace I saw in the eyes that had formerly been so haunted. He told us that he felt warm inside, in his heart, and that he could still feel the loving connection with his son. When our retreat came to its end, and all our good-byes were said, Joe walked out the front door to go home. He walked tall, toward a new horizon.

How to do Step Two:

1. Give yourself full permission to feel your pain and say your feelings out loud for twenty minutes (it might turn out to be shorter or longer than that).

2. Visualize the person you're forgiving in the empty chair, and allow your feelings to surface. Remind yourself that in this visualization, the person you are forgiving cannot hurt

you or walk out of the room while you vent your feelings. (It's only a chair!)

3. Imagine the person sitting there with a light over his or her head—the Higher Self, which is commanding the person to sit and listen to your feelings.

4. As you "observe" the person in the chair before you, sink your awareness into your body and contact the tension that arises inside you as you face this person. It may be a feeling of heaviness in your belly, an ache in your heart, or a lump stuck in your throat from your unexpressed emotions. Allow those physical sensations to become stronger, letting yourself "go there."

5. See which words, pictures, or memories are lodged inside you that need to be spoken aloud. Speak from those places in your body and mind. Speak the language of emotion: "I am deeply sad that you ..." "I hate you because ..." "F— you, George!" "You broke my heart when ..." "I remember when you ..." "I am devastated ..." "I was so humiliated when you ..." "You are such an idiot ..." (Foul language is appropriate when healing anger. It's also OK for you to be blaming, unreasonable, unfair, victim-y, vengeful, violent, and nonspiritual during Step Two. Let the person have it!)

6. Allow yourself to speak it all out, taking time for crying or venting anger as you go. There's no need to rush it or make yourself stop crying once you get started. It will stop on its own eventually.

7. Stay with this until you start to feel quiet inside and you have the sense that it's time to shift to the next thing. Then go on to Step Three.

Step Three: Release Expectations from Your Mind, One by One

There are a lot of things that you can't control in your life: the weather, the economy, and the attitudes and behavior of other people, to name a few. The ability to adjust or release your expectations about people and things as you go along is a life skill worth learning, and a hallmark of maturity. Perhaps you have lived long enough by now to realize that natural calamities like earthquakes, floods, and other "acts of God" are part and parcel of life on Earth, and you don't feel the need to blame anyone or resent things like this when they happen. You don't like them, but you know it's no use to judge them as "wrong" and remain attached to that judgment. When it comes to the flaws and foibles of other human beings (who are also part of Nature), however, we remain indignant and outraged. We fuss and fume and truly believe that they could and should be different than they are. How do we stop tormenting ourselves about what *people* do? How can we forgive other people for being bad and stupid and wrong when it is so clear to us how they *should* behave?

I think we hold on to expectations of others for a very long time because our expectations seem very reasonable to us, just part of a "norm" that we assume is good and necessary. It takes a while for us to accept that these people or situations really are the way they are; some things are so *wrong* to us that we find it hard to believe that people are not going to see the light soon and change for the better. It feels *wrong* to us to let go of our reasonable expectations of other people even when we continue to see evidence that someone cannot or will not meet them.

Another reason it feels counterintuitive to release our expectations of other people is that "society" is almost by definition a web of mutually understood, healthy expectations that constitute a group consensus of what is "normal." We expect people to obey red lights and to wear appropriate clothing to work. We expect our mates to be faithful to us and to share or support our goals. Your job description is the list of expectations your employer has of you, and your satisfactory performance on the job is a condition of your being employed in that role in that company. Healthy expectations in society are based on mutual agreements that healthy people make with each other and live by, fairly harmoniously.

What do we do when a person cannot or will not meet some of our healthy expectations? What if they are not mature or mentally stable enough to keep certain agreements? Depending on the situation, the options before you might include:

- Release your unrealistic expectations and start afresh, with right-sized expectations and a willingness to see the good.
- Release your expectations of someone in order to regain your goodwill, but restate your expectations to them about what you will and will not allow in your relationship.
- Release your expectation that your employee should have avoided a big mistake, but reprimand or fire the person.
- Release your expectation that your boss be fair or pleasant, but continue to do what is required of you because you need the job. Or, release your expectation that your boss be fair or pleasant, and look for a new job.

- Release your expectation that your drunk uncle should have behaved well at Thanksgiving dinner last year but don't invite him to Thanksgiving again.
- Release your expectation that your friend who is afflicted with bipolar disorder is easy to be with when she's in a manic cycle, but visit her for shorter amounts of time.
- Release your expectation that your spouse understands you, but stay and make the best of things. Or, release your expectation that your spouse understands you, and divorce him.
- Forgive someone who cheated you, but sue the person in court.
- Forgive your teenager for breaking the rules, but continue to hold her to the rules, because it is still your important responsibility to teach her and help her manage herself.

Why do forgiveness and releasing expectations keep making it onto the list of what to do? Because I'm still making the case to you to *forgive everyone and everything*. It's very important to understand that the act of forgiveness does not assume that we will remain in a relationship that does not work for us in fundamental ways. But forgiveness is something that you *always* do for yourself, in order to let go of the impact of a hurt. The worldly action and boundary adjustments are a separate matter.

There are some general expectations that we have about others that get us into trouble all the time, and many of our problems with people fall within these categories:

- We expect them to share our important values.
- We expect them to keep promises and agreements.
- We expect them to be as mature as we are.
- We expect them to want the same things in relationships that we do.
- We expect them to be sane and to act "normal."

Sharing values

It is natural for us to prefer that other people share our important values. We are inspired and comfortable with people who are like us and embody what we think is good and admirable. We are a little awkward and uncomfortable relating to people whose values are very different from ours. Most of us were raised within a value system, whether it was strongly delineated for us by our elders or just subtly all around us like the wallpaper or the air we breathed. We imbibed and incorporated our families' values and behaviors both consciously and unconsciously, and some of these "norms" continued to define our expectations of others when we became adults. Our values also grow strongly out of our life experiences, and they are reflections of what we treasure for good citizenship: being fair and honest; working hard; being devoted to our spouses and children; or being Republicans, Democrats, Christians, vegetarians, or feminists.

Sometimes we identify with our values so strongly that we forget other people have a right to be different, and that these "different" people are actually the same as us on a deeper level. If you usually become annoyed with your brother-in-law every year at a family gathering because of your differing political views, you have the choice to remain annoyed each year or to release your expectation that he thinks the same way you do. If you take some time the week before and preemptively vent your feelings about your differences, you will be able to say, *I release my expectation that my brother-in-law will agree with me about what kind of job the president is doing. I am willing to focus on our commonalities.* If you sincerely do this, you will have a fresh view of him as a person. You can notice instead, *He is a passionate and strong person. The turkey stuffing is amazing this year. The kids are being hilarious.* As you focus on these commonalities, however small, you will enjoy harmony with him at the next holiday dinner instead of conflict.

Promises and agreements

If one of our family members breaks an important agreement (for example: committing sexual infidelity, gambling, lying, stealing, or hiding the use of substances), we have to make the painful decision about whether we will remain in the relationship or end it because our trust is completely broken. For a while, at least, we need to redraw the line that says how far we are able to trust the person. Though it is difficult to end an active relationship with someone in the family, the truth is we are always free to make choices about how we relate to her, or if we do. We can give her another chance, decide not to see her anymore, or even sue her in court, if it is a legal offense and that is what is called for. But whatever we choose, if we do it consciously with a goal of ultimate forgiveness, we will release the stain of that hurt and disappointment on our hearts and not sully other relationships with residual suspicion and mistrust.

Different levels of maturity

Oftentimes, we have to release the expectation that another person is as mature as we are. Some people just *don't get it*, we think, as we watch them act out in blatant disregard for the good of others and for the good of a whole situation. It is frustrating to watch an immature person make a mistake that hurts others. People who are immature are often selfish and cannot be counted on to be wise, for their selfishness makes them *unable* to take the overall situation into account as they make important decisions.

This scenario is especially exasperating if a "young soul," so to speak, is in a leadership position, like a parent, a boss, or the president. They wield power without wisdom, causing unnecessary harm. It is hard to allow people in power to go through their learning processes, especially when they are making a big mess that hurts others. Sometimes our hands are tied, or our own power to influence the situation is limited. We have to just witness the unhappy scenario as it unfolds, playing only the part that is given to us to play, as best as we can. We can only hope that somehow, in the long term, things will right themselves for everyone again.

I worked with a woman named Alice who needed to forgive a man in charge of a large downsizing and restructuring in the health care corporation that she worked for. She worked as a doctor in a family practice clinic that had enjoyed very little staff turnover for nearly twenty years. Alice loved going to work every day, and she served some of the same families for years and years—she knew she was valuable and trusted. Alice loved the warm, productive hum of that stable and cooperative work group: they were accustomed to each other's needs and rhythms and attentive to each other's well-being and life passages. It was that rare treasure in the world of employment—a satisfying job and a fine working unit that cared about its members. It fulfilled her need to be part of a meaningful community, every day.

Although the clinic was stable and well organized, economic times were hard and the clinic was not exempt from the HMO's top-down mandate to cut expenses by 35 percent, *ASAP*. The executives hired a "hatchet man" to carry out the unpleasant task. A tiny man, drunk with power, Ed was fresh from a previous job in which he had felt disrespected. He seemed intoxicated with the authority he was given in his new job, and so he threw his weight around willfully, almost gleefully ignoring the personal human element in all that he did. He made generalized, hardline decisions that literally destroyed the caring culture of the medical clinic, which had been in place for nearly two decades. He ignored suggestions from experienced managers and swept positions away without careful thought. He let experienced people go instead of attempting to reposition them, losing the value of their experience in the new situation.

Ed used the classic "pink slip" approach. In the middle of the clinic day, he informed health workers—including Alice—that he was letting them go, *now*, and told them to clean out their desks while a security guard stood by to prevent them from stealing anything. Then the guard escorted these dedicated, responsible people outside, leaving them shocked, humiliated, and suddenly bereft of their jobs and their work community. They weren't even allowed, legally, to say good-bye to long-term patients. "It isn't personal," Ed said to fine clinicians who had brought their hearts to their work for years. The way Ed carried out this downsizing and restructuring hurt so many people, and it could have been so different if he'd had more wisdom. Even though the clinic remained where it was and continued to operate, it lost its "center" as an organization and was never the same. Two years after this teardown occurred, Ed was fired and moved along. Alice felt that he left in his wake a ruined, broken shell of what the clinic had been before.

Ten years after Ed rudely rushed her out of her job, Alice still carried the hurt of that cruel loss in her heart. She felt like she had witnessed a happy village being mowed down by vicious mercenaries, and she grieved the loss of the wholeness that she had known in her work life back then. She moved on into two other jobs that were OK, but she still walked around in a mild depression after that job loss. Alice came to see me because she was ready for a change and knew intuitively that she could not create something truly satisfying again until she forgave the experience of losing the job where she had been so happy. She found relief by letting go of two big expectations: (1) that her former superior was wise and mature and would conduct the restructuring in a caring and respectful way, and (2) that the happy era she had known at the clinic could have continued into the present day. When she got through this issue, she was at peace. Although she would always believe that Ed's leadership was flawed and his actions were wrong, she let the sad story go and was ready to start fresh with her goal to create a satisfying work life again.

Forgiving the immaturity of teenagers

Another common instance in which expectations cause problems is when parents must forgive the immaturity of their teenagers as they pass through the whitewater rapids of the teen years. Teenage children are too big to completely control and too inexperienced to be wise. We helplessly watch them make mistakes while they insist that they know what they are doing. They wish that we wouldn't tell them what to do so often, but don't they know we *must* still guide them? No. They just don't realize how young they still are. Current brain research reveals that teenagers' brains are still in a phase of rapid and complex development that continues until they are over twenty years old. The frontal lobe, the part of the brain that influences judgment, is in a highly plastic and developmental state all through the teen years. It allows teens to learn new things quickly, but it doesn't yet have the solid links between actions and consequences. That missing piece of teenage brain function is the cause of so much stress for worried parents. Though it is stressful for everyone concerned, it is actually the process of making mistakes and learning from them that causes the brain to develop more of these connections. In other words, mistakes are one of the building blocks of a person's maturity. Great! But it's a harrowing time. Personally, I think the age of seventeen is the worst, because many children that age are like miserable birds molting their feathers—too big to be happy in the nest and too young to fly away, they sullenly sit with droopy wings, their eyes accusing us, *You are wrong; leave me alone*. It's hard to feel like we're getting it right as parents when our children are in that transition. We all just have to get through that time with our best judgment, until it passes and our children are older and wiser.

What peace there is for parents of teens comes with our ability to release our expectations: that they should be mature enough to *get it* right now, or that they should trust our wise advice to them the first time instead of messing up. We have to hold to our rules and limits and guiding role even while they may dislike us, releasing the expectation that family life is easy these days. If we are able to be realistic in our expectations of the maturing process, and not require that it be sane and orderly, we will be able to greet each learning crisis with serenity.

How to do Step Three:

1. Prepare yourself to distill all of your emotional expression into a few pithy statements of the positive things you had been expecting from the person you're forgiving. It might be helpful to write them down and then cross them off as you complete each one.

2. In addition to your specific situation, notice if you had been expecting shared values, maturity, or sanity from this person.

3. State your first expectation as a positive preference: "I would have preferred that you would have been honest with me..."

4. Acknowledge reality: "but you weren't . . ."

5. Restate your will: "and I will not hold on to this anymore."

6. Cancel out your expectation with a firm statement: "Therefore, I release my expectation that you should have been

honest with me." (Use a sweeping motion with your hand, if you wish.)

7. Go inside yourself and release that one expectation. Close your eyes, breathing softly and compassionately into the place in your body where you had held that expectation. It's usually the heart and/or the belly, but it could also be the throat or head. Imagine your attachment to that one expectation dissolving. Let your own imagery for releasing this block come to you. (Examples: ice melting and becoming water, something solid breaking up into little pieces of dust and being swept away, a fist unclenching, or a knot of energy inside you untying and flowing freely.)

8. When you feel neutral, or there is more quiet and open space inside you, go on to the next expectation in the same way, until you have addressed them all.

9. Then go on to Step Four or Step Five, in either order. (The next two steps, Restore Your Boundaries and Open up to the Universe to Get Your Needs Met in a Different Way, can be done in whatever order feels more natural for your process. For simplicity's sake, I have named them Step Four and Step Five, but do them in whatever order feels right to you.)

Step Four: Restore Your Boundaries

Step Four is very liberating. It is the point in the forgiveness process when we firmly separate ourselves from the wrong actions and attitudes of the other person. The act of restoring our boundaries with another has two parts to it: on a moral level, we give the person full responsibility for the consequences of his or her actions and attitudes, and on a subtle energy level, we reinforce our individual "personal space," the protective field of life force around us known as the *aura*.

What are "boundaries"? A boundary is the defining line that determines what is ours and what isn't, and what we will and will not do. Our boundaries are the verbal or nonverbal declarations of what we will and will not allow to happen to us, and how we want to use our time and energy—they are a natural outgrowth of our values and our current intentions. On a physical level, we easily recognize boundaries. They are the fences around our properties, the locks on our doors, and the way we share or do not share our money and our valued possessions. In the workplace, we speak of boundaries when we talk about being *professional* or *unprofessional*. At work, our clothing and our manners communicate a certain amount of *containment*, symbolic ways of saying, *I am in a work role now; I am managing my time and focus, and I expect others to respect that too*. In most professional circumstances, we are emotionally contained, not displaying the full range of our feelings or allowing personal upsets to be dramatically visible to our colleagues. We take those feelings to a private conversation with a friend or a therapist. We have different behaviors and ways of expressing ourselves— different boundaries—at work than we do when we are out having fun with our best buddies. We are talking about physical and social boundaries when we say things like:

- *Can you believe how inappropriate that was?*
- *It's probably not my business, but—*
- *Back off! That is not your business.*
- *That's enough. No more, please.*

- *No, I'm sorry, I can't help you.*
- *I don't like how flirtatious she was being toward my husband.*
- *Too much information! I don't want you to tell me those very personal things.*
- *He made advances with me on our first date, and I wasn't ready. I won't see him again.*

Physical and social boundaries are easier to recognize than emotional and mental ones.

When we obsess, overreact, worry, or mentally attempt to control the future or other people's opinions of us, we have lost our boundaries. When we are in "right relationship" with our boundaries, we take responsibility for what is ours and let go of everything else, just letting it be. Mental and emotional boundaries may be the most important of all, because they are the ones that help us to be "comfortable in our own skin." We have lost our mental or emotional boundaries when we say things like:

- I can't stop thinking about the nerve of that guy.
- I worry all the time about ...
- I'm afraid that others will think I'm too ...
- That meeting gave me a stress headache.
- I feel so sorry about her problem; I couldn't sleep last night thinking about the pain she is going through.

We can't take the mistakes, problems, emotions, or judgments of others into our personal spaces as if they were ours, or we will be quite uncomfortable. That is a loss of our boundaries, and it isn't healthy for us or for others. Of course we have to stretch ourselves uncomfortably at times for those who truly are our responsibility, like our children and our aging parents, but everyone else in our lives can likely fend for themselves. We can kindly offer our input, help, and compassion when we perceive it is needed, or if people ask for it, as long as it is practical for us to do so. The free and generous help we offer another person should fit within the overall balance of our lives; our healthy level of involvement is dictated by our time, energy, goals, and other responsibilities.

In the first part of Step Four (Restore Your Boundaries), you give the person you are forgiving full responsibility for his actions. You clearly draw the line between yourself and him and imagine yourself handing back over to him his pile of mistakes and wrongdoings. *This is your stuff,* you say, *I will no longer carry it around inside me;* or *Not my problem, I'm letting it go;* or *This is all your own bad karma to deal with, not mine*—you get the idea. You give yourself the gift of significantly "lightening up" when you release the false responsibility for another that you have taken on.

In the second part of Step Four, you heal and reinforce your healthy personal space, sometimes called your *aura*. (Note to the reader: you may or may not be familiar with this concept of auras, and I will explain it as I understand and have experienced it in my work as simply as possible here. For more information, please see Appendix F, "Notes on the Subtle Energy System," on page 185.) The aura is a subtle energetic field surrounding you, usually about three feet out from your body. Those who can see energy see it as a bubble of colored light around a person, and it is most visible around the head. It's your own quality-controlled energetic environment, within which is held the energy of your own thoughts, emotions, and physical vitality. A good, strong aura is a reflection of your healthy self-concept and the power with which you are able to have your own thoughts, feelings, and intentions, especially when you are in the company of other people. It is a filter: it buffers the impact of people and environments that are not appropriate for you, and it lets in things that are good. It allows you to pass through a variety of human environments (the office, the mall, the traffic jam) without taking in the stress of a lot of chaotic energy.

A naturally strong auric field is also your protector, because it communicates silently to others: *Don't mess with me; I don't allow it.* I am sure that street thieves are adept at reading the auras of potential marks, whether they realize they are looking at energy fields or not. If you were not taught or helped to define your self and your personal space while growing up, you might have a weak auric field, a reflection of your weak sense of who you are. A weak aura is very permeable, letting in too much energy from other people and environments. This is the aura of a person who can't say no to others, and that weakness shows subtly all around the person. People with weak, permeable energy boundaries are easily overwhelmed by noisy or chaotic environments; they can't stay long in a crowd, because it feels like too much.

From my experience working with people who were violated or traumatized by others, I get the strong impression that the aura, or subtle energy boundary, is compromised by the wound and receives a hole or a rip in it. This injury to the aura can keep one vulnerable to similar kinds of use and abuse by others again and again until it is "mended" by a healing process. The best medicine for this problem is forgiveness of the original violation or trauma. Because many victims erect a wall around themselves, desperately trying to avoid this kind of pain again, it seems counterintuitive to forgive the people who hurt them. The idea that forgiving the offender is the key to finding empowerment and safety again seems ludicrous, but I promise you it is really the truth. If you have a *wall* instead of a *boundary*, it keeps everything out—even joy, love, and new opportunities. And it doesn't even work that well to protect you from repeat offenses, because of that weak spot.

A healthy boundary, on the other hand, has its own intelligence, and when it is in place and functioning well, it serves as an amazing source of comfort and protection. It lets love and good energy in to nourish you, and filters inappropriate energy out. Your aura grows stronger with forgiveness, as old inner wounds are mended and your sense of self grows stronger. It grows firmer and stronger with discriminating use of the word "no" and with the wise demarcation of what is yours and what is not, day by day. What does a healthy energy boundary feel like? Here are a few ways I've heard it described:

- "I feel safe. It's like I'm in a protective bubble, and I feel calm and connected."
- "I feel strong and aware, in charge of what I do and how I interact with people."
- "I feel detached around my sister's problems. She says the same things now that used to drive me crazy, but it's like her words just slide off me and don't 'stick.'"
- "The person that I forgave seemed to have so much power over me before I forgave him. Now he is smaller and more at a distance from me, not filling up my head anymore. I can see him as separate from me—we are not tangled up with each other."
- "My ex-husband used to say cruel and critical things to me; it felt like his words slammed into my heart and stomach and made me feel sick inside. When he came once a week to pick up our son for a visit, he'd usually say something mean to me that affected me for the rest of the day. After I forgave him, I felt my energy boundary drop into place around me, very palpably—it was so surprising! The next time he came, his words didn't get anywhere

near my heart; it's like my boundary was a powerful, invisible defender that protected me by destroying the bad energy of his words before it could hit me—the negativity in his words melted away into the air before it got anywhere close. I've stopped reacting to him, and after so many years, he's stopped talking to me that way, because I no longer give him the satisfaction of reacting. We still don't like each other, but since we have to cooperate around the shared custody of our son, we have to still see each other each week. At least he comes and goes peacefully now."

How to do Step Four:

1. Give the person you're forgiving responsibility for his or her actions and attitudes. Use body language to symbolize giving back the person's "stuff" to him or her. Set all the remaining debris concerning that person's actions clearly outside of your space, at least three feet away from you. Firmly state, out loud, "I give you full responsibility for all your actions and attitudes."

2. Reestablish and strengthen your personal space by visualizing a healthy energetic boundary (your aura). Visualize a bubble of light around you—a smooth, egg-shaped container, which protects you and filters out energy and concerns that are not yours.

3. As you visualize this aura, breathe into it and imagine it is filling with colored light, installing a safe space and a healthy boundary. You can pick a favorite color or see what color comes to you intuitively. Clearly see the other person farther away from you, with your energies now separate. Go on to Step Five.

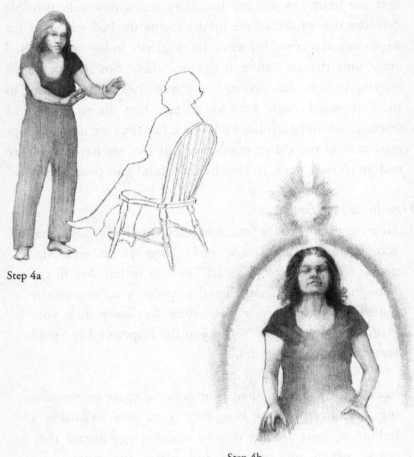

Step 4a

Step 4b

Step Five: Open up to the Universe to Get Your Needs Met in a Different Way

Very often, if we are attached to an expectation and stubbornly unable to let it go, it is because we are unconsciously trying to get an important need met, and it is that frozen need inside us that drives our judgments and makes demands of other people. In other words, we rigidly demand certain behaviors from another because those behaviors symbolize something important to us and our sense of wholeness. What we don't realize is that we can actually loosen up on our specific demands and expectations of others and ask the Universe to take care of our needs. It may be a reasonable, present-time need, or it may be something unfulfilled and frozen inside us from when we were growing up.

Joan and her husband always got in a fight when it came time to make a joint financial decision. Though they were usually amiable together, as soon as they had a discussion that involved math or money, the tension rose and the gloves came off. Joan said Steve was bossy and didn't listen to her. Steve said Joan was pushy and she wasn't making any sense—where were the facts to support her choice to do something? This made her feel dismissed as "a stupid female" and only enraged her further. The fights usually resolved with one person sullenly giving way to what the other wanted, but nobody was ever happy. They always felt tense with each other for a few days after their money fights.

One day Joan sat down to forgive Steve for being so bossy and treating her like she was stupid. Soon she found herself in a memory of being treated as if she were "a stupid female" by a male math teacher when she was in fourth grade. She had so much anger inside her from long ago, as well as a fear that she was not smart when it came to math and money. How much of the problem was Steve's actual "bossiness," and how much was him reacting to Joan's own fear and anger projected outward to him? They were both fighting with something that had nothing to do with Steve. Joan went to work clearing out this old issue, and the next time she talked to Steve, he was so much more reasonable! Her desperate attachment to winning her point in the argument melted away as she began to let the Universe meet her real need: *an inside sense of security about her own intelligence.* She was less defensive and more sure of herself, and her growing confidence in herself helped Steve to relax and trust Joan's ideas more. She also became willing to gather more of the facts that Steve needed to hear in order to be comfortable with her ideas. Their money issue resolved itself.

The Universe wants all of us to thrive. There is a force of restoration afoot in the Universe that is intelligent and, at times, very creative! I see this all the time at the forgiveness weekend workshop—especially in the synchronistic way in which certain individuals are attracted to this time and place, and how they have something special to share with each other. The kind of invisible orchestration that goes on at the level of Spirit is simply hard to get your mind around some days. I guess that's why they say, "God speaks in miracles."

Sara was an attendee at the workshop who came with a clear intention to forgive her father. A woman with a laser-like mind and good business sensibilities, she wanted to bring some attention to her heart and to heal the bleak depression-around-the-edges that was always with her. She struggled with a tendency to overwork, and her choice to come to the workshop was a step in the direction of some new balance in her life. Sara grew up on a farm, and her father worked all the time. He was a stern, joyless individual who used his children like slaves on the farm. They all had to work hard on the farm after school, and except for home-work, every minute of their time was used for work. The children had no time for play or daydreaming, and their father never gave them any loving affection or took time for some fun together. Sara was a friendly, sociable girl, and she often felt sad that she could not stay in town after school and hang out with the other girls or attend parties and social events. She especially wanted to be a Girl

Scout and go to meetings in a smart green uniform. She longed to wear the sash full of badges that the Girl Scouts wore to mark their accomplishments. She was clever and ambitious, and she imagined wearing a sash with the most badges in the town! But it was not to be—her father expected her to come home to muck out the barn, bring in the cows, help her mother put up preserves, and so on. She worked alone or with her brothers every day after school and felt like her real life as an individual was passing her by, lost forever.

As I guided her through the Eight Steps, Sara spoke to her father in the empty chair and cried her eyes out about her lost girlhood and her oppressive experience on the family farm. She also yelled at him for being empty of anything except his work ethic. She stated her preference that she could have had a life that was more balanced in work and play, and that she could have been a Girl Scout. Then she released it all. As we mused together afterward about the positive results of her childhood experience, she cited her strong work ethic, and we imagined what some of her life's accomplishments would look like as symbolic badges on a sash.

Then the Universe swung into gear to give Sara what she needed. That night, another attendee named Gloria went up to her attic to retrieve a carefully preserved Girl Scout uniform that she had saved for forty years. It was just Sara's size! The sash was heavy with the bright, carefully sewn badges. She ironed the green dress lovingly and brought it to the workshop the next day. Gloria conspiratorially whisked Sara away with her into the ladies' room, and as we brought the group together to begin the day, the doors in the back of the room banged open. Gloria announced, "Ta-dah!" as Sara the Girl Scout marched in, dressed in full regalia: green dress, cap, knee socks, saddle shoes, and the sash full of honor badges. The room erupted in victory shouts and standing applause as Sara skipped down the aisle to prance around in front of us, her eyes sparkling. I swear, she looked like she was twelve. Sara the Girl Scout was with us for the rest of the day, and it was rewarding to see her be so light and girlish; she was already a more balanced and joyful person than the earnest, hard-working businesswoman who had walked in on Friday night. Gloria allowed Sara to keep the uniform for as long as she wanted, until her need for it was completely fulfilled.

How to do Step Five:

1. As you sit there, imagine being completely unattached to the person you are forgiving; there are no longer any needs or "strings" connecting you to him or her.

2. With a trusting heart and a wide open mind, open your hands and extend them upward, asking the Universe to help you get your needs met in a different way. Visualize a channel that connects you to the Universe's gifts and resources, like a funnel that opens out into the Universe. Be willing to have good new experiences in the near future. Go on to Step Six.

Step Six: Receive Spirit's Healing Energy into Your Personality

In religious terms, it is often said that God's forgiveness is given to us freely for the asking, and that His Light and His healing are always available for us. I believe that is true, but what is also true is that most of us are unable to receive God's forgiveness, to take that healing inside and utilize the light and energy that

comes from God to heal our issues. Most of us are so encased in the defensive shell of the ego, and our inner spaces are so blocked up with emotional congestion, that God could be aiming a fire hose of light right at us, and we wouldn't get it. The healing energy stops at that hard shell all around us and streams away from us, leaving us untouched and miserable.

The gift of the Eight Steps to Freedom is that we are able to use the first five steps as *preparation to become able* to receive some grace and light from a higher level. By deciding to open up, and by venting our emotions and combing out our mental expectations, it's like we have gone in there and broken up a hard formation of cement into little chunks and pieces. Then there is a little room inside us to be open and ready for the energy from our Higher Self to pour into us like water, rinsing away that debris and leaving us feeling fresh and new inside, with a sort of emptiness that is a positive feeling of peace.

In Step Six, you reach to the higher level and bring unconditional love and light down from there into your personality, or human self. Visualize your soul, which is a globe of light hovering overhead, a part of the greater field of light that is Spirit, or the Universe. Imagine that you can open a "skylight" at the top of your head and let the light flow down into your head and then throughout your *physical body*, cleansing and renewing you. From the point of view of an energy healer, what you are doing here is drawing light and soulful energy from the *transpersonal chakra* that hovers over your head, down through the *crown chakra* at the top of the head, infusing your whole being (see Appendix F, "Notes on the Subtle Energy System," on page 185). This new, vital energy enters each of the chakra centers, which then distribute that vitality throughout your *subtle energy body*. Then you bring the light into your emotional body, nurturing your heart and self with love and affection. Last, the light goes into your mind, your *mental body*, bringing peace, quiet, and detachment. In Step Six, love and light fill you, in all of the levels of your being, until you feel empty of the issue and full of peace.

Something physical actually happens when you imagine bringing the light down from the center above your head into your personality. It feels different to different people:

- "My whole head filled up with light, and I felt like I was being restored by a Presence."
- "I feel it like cool, tingly water pouring in from above, rinsing me clean."
- "The light is warm and golden-white, and it pours slowly and thickly into me like honey."
- "I feel tingly from head to foot, and very fresh and energized."
- "I know the light is coming into me because my mind goes silent, and I feel quiet and very neutral—in simple harmony with everything."

How to do Step Six:

1. Sit upright, eyes closed.

2. Visualize a globe of light, like a sun, hovering above your head (twelve to eighteen inches up). The light of that sun is shining with love and healing energy.

3. Imagine that you can open up the top of your head, your crown center, like a skylight. The energy of light and love from your Higher Self pours down into your personality, systematically clearing your physical body, your emotions, your subtle energy body, and your mind.

4. The light pours into your body, bringing calm, release, and new vitality.

5. The light pours into your seven chakra centers, which then distribute that vital energy throughout your entire subtle energy body.

6. The light pours into your heart, belly, and feeling self, bringing a sense of being loved, valued, comforted, and assured.

7. The light pours into your mind, bringing calm detachment, emptiness, and openness to a new experience.

8. When you feel calm and cleansed, go on to Step Seven.

Step Seven: Send Unconditional Love to the Other Person and Release Him or Her

In Step Seven, you allow the light flowing through you from a higher level to extend outward to the person you are forgiving. As much as it is desirable to be loved by other people, it is even more important that we are able to love others to some degree. It is healthy for you to have the stream of universal love flowing in you, through you, and out to others at all times. Once you learn to love like this, you can love *anyone*, a little, even someone who has wronged you, even a difficult person who does not love you back. The unconditional love from Spirit is all-inclusive, extending itself freely to all people and all of Creation, regardless of . . . anything! It puts us right with life because, for whatever reason, the person or thing we're forgiving has its place in Creation, just as we do, and we need to accept that. We don't have to like everyone, but we can still have goodwill for them as citizens of the Universe. We can send light and goodwill from our souls to their souls and release them, which also releases us from them. This is a blessed relief. And mysteriously, as we make things right between us on the soul level, things start to right themselves on the personality level too. We are all connected, all the time. If you shift your attitude toward someone from resentment to goodwill, *even at a distance*, the person feels it and starts to change his or her attitude with you too.

Larry came to see me because he desperately needed to forgive his mother, who had behaved in a cruel and rejecting way toward him for many years. His mother lived far away, in New York City, and he only talked to her by phone about twice a year. That's all the contact he could tolerate, because every time they spoke, she was verbally abusive and put him down, telling him again and again she thought he was a terrible disappointment as a son. He felt emotionally devastated every time they spoke, suffering from dark depressions and a tendency to use substances in an attempt to medicate his pain. Now he had been diagnosed with a terminal illness and was determined to "clean things up" inside him. He quit using and decided to forgive his mother, because he needed to be free and at peace with himself, now more than ever. He hoped he could love her just because she was his mom and gave him life.

Larry was ripe for this session with me, because he had spoken to his mother on the phone the night before, and she was as awful as ever. He cried deeply with anguish about his mother's rejection of him throughout his life. He cried and cried, releasing his lonely shame and despair, and eventually he was ready to move through the steps of forgiveness, letting go of the expectation that she would ever like and accept him. He restored his boundaries, giving her the responsibility for her failed relationship with him and filling his space with vibrant purple light and the energy of unshakable self-love. At the end, Larry sent his negative old mother a brilliant blessing of unconditional love and light, a spiritual triumph that freed him at last. He was beautifully at peace as he left my office.

That night, a miracle happened. Larry's mother called him up from New York City, a surprise call because they had just spoken and he didn't expect to hear from her for another six months. But this time his mother's voice was different; it was a humble voice from a mother he knew long ago and barely remembered. "Larry," she said, "I realized today that when I talked to you on the phone last night I was mean, and that I usually talk to you this way. I don't know why I do it, Larry. And it's not right. And ... I'm really sorry. Next time I'll do better."

What happened here? It was the ordinary miracle of two human beings getting right with each other because one of them decided to forgive the other. It only takes one person to set the stage for this miracle to happen. Sometimes the change is instantaneous, and sometimes it takes a while, but it's successful world peace work at the most intimate level.

How to do Step Seven:

1. With the light still flowing into you from Spirit, extend your hands in blessing to the person you have forgiven.

2. Visualize a continuous stream of God's light flowing down to you and out your hands to the other person, wherever he or she is.

3. Say out loud, "I send you this Higher Love, _____, and I release you to be yourself. And I release myself from you." You can symbolize this with a hand gesture too, if you wish. (Note: if it is too hard to send love to the person because he or she has been abusive, or you dislike the person intensely, visualize the light going directly from your Higher Self to that person's Higher Self, avoiding the personality level completely.)

4. Visualize the two of you, now separate on a personal level
   (in your own distinct, separate spaces) but connected on the
   spiritual level by a bridge of light. Then go on to Step Eight.

Step Eight: See the Good in the Person or Situation

The last step to forgiving another person brings you back to a
simple way of expressing unconditional love: see the good in the
person and choose to focus on that instead of those other things
you don't like. It's the good old "glass half-full instead of half-
empty" idea. It may sound Pollyanna-ish, but this new habit will
give you peace and rest at last. Everyone has something good
about her, if you look for it. If necessary, you can select some
small, superficial thing to like about the person, to give your
mind something to do besides obsessing about larger character
defects. Maybe your villain has a nice smile, or looks good in red,
or is always prompt, or is very nice to his or her dog. There is
nothing too small or silly when it comes to finding some good to
focus on. Remember, you are doing this for yourself and your
own health.

Even my odious neighbor Angie has several admirable qualities: (1) she always has her nails done beautifully, (2) she puts
pots of flowers on her steps, and (3) she bakes cookies for her
grandchildren. Those are good things, yes? I personally don't do
any of those things with any consistency. So what if she's not
friendly? Superficial things aside, I have come to admire Angie
because I see that she has an amazing capacity for endurance; if
half the rumors I've heard about her are true, she's survived a hell
of a lot. When I do see her or think of her, I either feel neutral,
or I feel a little strand of goodwill and respect for her even
though I don't like her. In other words, there's no problem now.

As you get used to forgiving people as a way of life, it becomes less and less important whether you like someone or not.

Edith modeled this process for me one time when she was facilitating forgiveness for a woman in her workshop who forgave her boss. The woman—I'll call her Rose—felt lighter and better, but when they got to Step Eight, she had a hard time seeing the good in him.

It went like this:

Edith: What is good about him?

Rose: Nothing! There's nothing at all good about him! He's just a terrible person.

Edith: Nothing at all? Are you sure?

Rose: I'm positive. There's nothing good about him at all.

Edith: Well, when he comes to work, does he wear clothes?

Rose (bewildered): Of course—of *course* he wears clothes to work.

Edith: Well that's good, isn't it?

Sometimes it's really a stretch. There may be a person in your life who has been so terrible to you that it seems impossible to see the good in him or her. If you don't want to settle for merely being glad that the person wears clothes in public, you can get more serious about discovering what good has come out of your situation and what kind of character strength you had to develop or express in order to deal with this person. Now your job is to put these few simple good thoughts in your brain as you walk into the future without your previous distress.

How to do Step Eight:

1. Think of a few good things about the person you have forgiven, and say them out loud. (Examples: He has a nice smile. She is a hard worker. He is really funny.)

2. If you can't think of anything good about the person, think of something good that the situation brought to you. Or think of a character strength you had to develop because you had to deal with this person and situation. (Examples: I became stronger. I learned to be more compassionate. I learned to ask for help. I felt closer to God.)

3. Remind yourself that this good thing is what you intend to remember and focus on whenever you think of this person or situation in the future.

Self-mastery challenge! Take Step Eight even further by spreading good rumors

Step Eight may seem simplistic, but it isn't. It's powerful, if you are committed to it. Unconditional love, even on an elementary level, works wonders. If you want to experiment with the efficacy of this universal law, take Step Eight even further by spreading good rumors about the person you used to be angry at. Chances are he has alienated a few other people in your community, and the group has attached some negativity to him, which keeps his and the

community's dynamics in a certain negative pattern. Watch what happens if *you* forgive him and then spread a positive point of view to others instead of negative gossip. We are all connected; when one person shifts away from negativity, and helps others to do so, a strange, positive alchemy takes place that helps even an intractable person find the support in the Universe to make a needed change. I dare you to try this.

How to spread good rumors about a problematic person:

1. Make a list of everything, no matter how small, that is good about the problematic person.

2. Memorize this list, and incorporate this point of view into your heart so that you can easily bring it to mind.

3. When a natural opportunity arises, plant one of these appreciative ideas in conversation with a mutual acquaintance. For example: "Do you know what I really like about George? He is always well prepared and on time for meetings." (Instead of saying, "George is oppositional in every meeting.")

4. The next time you can, speak a good rumor to another person about George, choosing a different one from the list. "Have you ever noticed that George has a knack for choosing good-looking ties to wear? I wonder where he shops."

5. Speak another one to a different person on another day: "Good old George. He's so clear about where he stands on things."

6. Spread good rumors about your problematic person, over time, as naturally as you can manage it, until you reach the end of your list.

What happened with the problem person in your group or community? Send me your story!

Integrate Your Change and Start Living in a New Way

If you have performed the Eight Steps to Freedom from this chapter thoroughly, you will be different. You have made a permanent change inside yourself that you need to get used to. Start by noticing the physical change that you have brought about. Take an inventory of yourself now, starting with your body. Most people report, "I feel lighter." Sometimes you feel lighter in a specific place, like your heart or your torso, and sometimes it's an all-over effect. Perhaps it is your breathing that is different, now fuller, softer, and deeper than before you started. "I can breathe now," people say. "I hadn't realized I wasn't breathing." You might observe that your shoulders are relaxed, or your tight stomach has uncurled. On an emotional level, you feel calm, neutral. Your mind is quiet and open in a new way. There might be a tingling sensation in your limbs, like your very cells are vibrating, or in your energetic body, which feels fresh and "shivery" as new energy circulates to places that were previously blocked and stagnant.

You are different now, and you will have to get used to your new way of being on all these levels—physically, emotionally, mentally, and energetically. If you were accustomed to waking up each day with a knot of tension in your stomach, or a soft cloud of sadness muffling your natural enthusiasm, it is (pleasantly) disorienting to wake up each day calm and open to the present moment instead. If you have been curled up around a problem for months or decades, it is very strange to walk forward without it. It is almost an "empty" feeling, but I encourage you to frame it as "clear." Embrace this emptiness as a positive state, a fresh new page, and slowly allow your soul to take up residence inside you, with new goals and daily behaviors.

I once worked with a man named Dennis whose physical change was so remarkable that he was pleasantly confused for about two weeks. He forgave his mother, who was terribly critical of him. He was her only child, and while he grew up, she watched him like a hawk and picked on him constantly. He felt scrutinized and "henpecked" all the time, and as an adult, he was hard on himself and a bit of a social misfit. Shy and jittery when he was with most people, Dennis always looked as if he was afraid of something. His manners were nervous and furtive, and he carried his shoulders up close to his ears in a defensive posture. Long after Dennis's mother had died, he lived each day still in reaction to her, as she was very much alive in his own head. Here he was, a man in his late forties who was a serious student of yoga philosophy, trapped inside the feelings and posture of a scared young boy.

During his forgiveness session, Dennis courageously released a lot of pain and anger about how his mother had treated him, and then he opened up to bringing in unconditional love and light from a higher level, for her and himself. As he did this, the patterns in his mind and in his emotions let go so much that it was like something melted in him, and his shoulders dropped from their frozen place into a more natural posture. He stood erect now, with his shoulders low and set back wide. This allowed his head to sit more comfortably on his body, no longer like a turtle's head about to pop back into its shell. He kept looking down at his arms, which swung long at his sides a few inches lower than they had used to. "I feel like my arms are too long!"

he said in bewilderment, moving his head gently around in its new position. "This feels really weird. And I feel ... peaceful? That is even weirder." Dennis was calm and clear-eyed, and there was no longer a hunted expression in the depths of his eyes. The real Dennis emerged, after decades of protective hiding. This new Dennis was a marvel to his friends, who had not known he was capable of calm self-assurance, which manifested now in hundreds of small ways in his daily life and interactions with others. It was miraculous.

Take it easy after a big piece of forgiveness work. This kind of healing is life-changing, so you need to integrate what happened, consciously, for at least several days afterward. You may continue to integrate your experience for some months to come, as you develop new behaviors, and your relationship to life and to others shifts into new and better patterns. For several days, it is wise to treat yourself like you're "post-op," as if you've had some outpatient surgery on your foot, and the doctor has instructed you to take it easy for a week. Take some time to be gentle with yourself because your subconscious and unconscious mind are still sorting things out and digesting this change. Your mind is closing out the past story and "rebooting" itself for the future.

Therefore, please don't do your big forgiveness work during an intense week at your workplace, or before an important meeting in which you want your brains to be sharp—you might be very unfocused and spaced out. Don't go to a loud restaurant right after your session, or to a family gathering, and don't try to talk to the person you forgave right away. You shouldn't run the risk of a contentious moment with the person while you are still putting your new attitude together. Get more rest than usual as you heal, and let this experience "gel." It's best to approach life gently until you feel very solid with your new attitude. Your behaviors are going to change too, and the behavior of others toward you. Take a few weeks, if necessary, to become accustomed to "a new normal."

How to integrate your change and start living in a new way:

1. Allow yourself the strange experience of being calm, empty, and peaceful in relation to this person or situation that used to bring stress. Allow some time to get used to "a new normal."

2. Take some personal time off for reflecting and staring into space.

3. Get some extra rest, so your subconscious and unconscious mind can sort things out in your dream state.

4. Spend some time in Nature.

5. Avoid any intense encounters with the person you've forgiven for several days.

6. When you think of the person or situation, "see the good." When you see the person again, remind yourself to focus on the good and allow her to be just the way she is.

7. If new irritations arise, instantly release your expectations as you go along. If you start to rev up into an avoidable conflict with someone you've already forgiven, refocus on one of the positive personal goals you have for yourself, and put your energy into that instead.

4

Self-Forgiveness: The Most Difficult Task of All Made Simple

Most people are very hard on themselves. During the first evening of my weekend intensive workshop, there is a poignant moment that invariably occurs. That is the moment when someone raises his or her hand and haltingly asks, "How do I forgive myself?" A simple enough question, to be sure, but the energetic subtext in this question is always so amazingly *heavy*. I can pal-pably feel the suffering behind that question, the despair that envelops it, and I notice that everyone in the room subtly leans forward and silently entreats, *Yes, how?*

In the journey of self-healing and spiritual illumination, self-forgiveness is the most difficult—and the most important—task of all. We create more pain and suffering around our own per-ceived failures and defects than anyone around us usually does. Some of us even torture ourselves mentally with silent verbal abuse. This is one of the worst forms of human cruelty, and it's not a crime of torture that the United Nations can ever address, because it is widespread and invisible. Millions of people walk around every day, mentally wounded and spiritually homeless, unable to find rest within themselves. After all, if you think something is wrong with you and can't show your own self a decent measure of acceptance and fond regard, where will you ever find peace in this world? The importance of healthy self-love cannot be overstated. Yet how does the uncomfortable person (shaped and reared by conditional love and society's narrow standards of success) release herself into a steady state of self-love? The answer lies with the truth that is found in the experience of self-forgiveness. If you make a commitment to seeking self-forgiveness whenever you feel bad about yourself, eventually you will get it and come to peace with yourself and the human situation.

How Is Self-Forgiveness Accomplished?

How, exactly, is self-forgiveness accomplished? It is accomplished swiftly and simply when you are ready for it, when you are tired of beating yourself up about a mistake or a character flaw, and you know you need to feel better. One day something inside you clicks into place and vehemently declares, *I am done with this! I have to stop beating myself up about this, right now!* Then you are ready. All you need to do is take some private time and some sacred space, away from the rest of your ordinary day, and make a date with your Higher Self—you will find It is already there waiting for you. Sit right down and honestly ask your Higher Self to forgive you completely for this specific issue. Lay out your suffering about the issue in detail, requesting help for mastering this difficult lesson in your life. Be brave and ask Spirit to completely remove this burden! Then continue along with the Steps of Self-Forgiveness, as they are outlined for you on pages 125–126. Simple. On the right day, when you sincerely go there, you will instantly receive great relief. It only takes about half an hour, and it will change your life.

How do you know that you are unhappy because of an issue that requires you to forgive yourself? There are certain obvious signs: continuous indulgence in a destructive addiction, depression, and thoughts or statements of self-loathing. It's not hard to see, in these cases, that you are punishing yourself. The question is, *why?* It's worth doing some inner investigation to discover what issue or issues in the back of your mind are driving this kind of self-torment. There are other obvious signs that you feel unworthy: the habit of not allowing others to be generous to you, or avoiding caring relationships that would enhance your life. Did you ever ask yourself why you deprive yourself of nice things? Just take a moment now to think of a few privileges and adventures that would be pleasurable, empowering, and just plain good for you. Is there any reason you don't do those things, except for the reason that you are still running low on self-love?

In her book *Guilt Is the Teacher, Love Is the Lesson,* Joan Borysenko gives us some more clues that may indicate you are unconsciously caught in guilt and shame: *I'm overcommitted. I really know how to worry. I'm a compulsive helper. I'm always apologizing for myself. I wake up anxious and can be anxious for weeks. I always blame myself. I worry about what other people think of me. I am not as good as people think I am. I'm a perfectionist. I hate to take any assistance or ask for any help. I can't say no.* If you are in the habit of one of these behaviors, you might be driven by a self-forgiveness issue.

Self-Forgiveness Issues
- You are generally disappointed in the shape of your life.
- You made a big mistake—or you made a big deal out of a little mistake.
- You don't like your body type.

- You are struggling with an addiction.
- You are in a ruined relationship.
- Your finances are a mess.
- You cannot live your own values.
- You feel guilty about not being a better parent.
- Your personality has a way of annoying other people.
- You have broken an agreement or let someone down.
- You have been mean or cruel to another person.
- Your emotions get the best of you.
- You become stuck in despair and depression.
- Your body is sick or aging, and you're facing mortality.
- You are dependent on others and wish you could be independent.
- You could not defend yourself from abuse as a child.
- You easily feel ashamed and unworthy.
- You fall short of your goals and dreams, all the time.

A brief word about guilt: guilt does have its upside. Healthy guilt is a function of your conscience, an uncomfortable prodding from within to make amends or to set something right. It is alleviated with right action, as well as self-forgiveness. But chronic guilt is unhealthy, usually installed by a toxic belief in a family system that teaches guilt like it's a virtue. That one's got to go! It responds fairly well to feedback from a (happy) friend and a sense of humor. There's plenty more that can be said about any of the above situations, but I want to focus here on three of them:

Shame, which is the hardest self-forgiveness issue

Falling Short, which is the most universal self-forgiveness issue

Emptiness, or the Neglected Heart, which is a widespread emotional problem that is rarely discussed

Let's talk about shame

Shame is an unhealthy and extremely toxic emotion that makes a person very sick inside. It plays out in families and in society in a self-destructive and violent way, and it is at the root of addiction as well as all forms of abuse. It is the psychological cause behind our society's overflowing jail cells and broken families. If we could heal the darkness of the shame that warps and distorts the health of individuals and groups of people all around us, we'd lay the groundwork for a whole new collective experience.

While guilty people feel they have done something bad or wrong, shame-filled people feel that who they are is bad and wrong. Shame says to us: *Who do you think you are? You're no good! You're unworthy and undeserving. The real you is defective, and you must hide your real self at all costs lest people see it and abandon you.* In a way, shame is a case of false identity, because it is like a core of darkness that lives inside us where the light of the soul should be. Instead of identifying ourselves with the strength and energy that is in our souls, we identify with the dark, broken identity that shame has created. We are disconnected from the light of our souls, even though it is right there, available to us at every moment. We spend an enormous amount of energy hiding from ourselves and from others.

People who are afflicted with shame have difficulty getting their needs met in life and in relationships, because they cannot accept their own needs. They cannot receive goodness, because they believe that they do not deserve anything. Shame-based people are afraid of intimacy, are socially isolated because they cannot bear the possibility of being seen, and cannot stand being challenged. They may be hypersensitive and defensive, unable to take even mild criticism from someone else because they generalize it to make their whole selves wrong. People who are unconsciously steeped in shame and a sense of worthlessness may be aggressive and attack others because they are projecting their own shame outward everywhere—trying to be the punisher instead of the punished. Shame is like a "hot potato" people toss to others, lest they be the ones caught being bad and wrong. What causes a person to be filled with shame?

There are many reasons that people become shameful, all of them rooted in hurtful experiences that were never healed: experiences of being overpowered, violated, or forced to do and be things that they didn't want to do or be. The worst cases involve interpersonal atrocities like physical or sexual abuse carried out by loved ones. Chances are those perpetrators are desperately caught in the cycle of shame themselves. They seek to release the internal pressure of shame from abuse they have endured by becoming perpetrators instead of victims, even though that release is temporary. Here are some examples of experiences that may cause shame:

- *Being exposed, laughed at, or humiliated by a more powerful person or a group:* being the target of the playground bully or the cruel teacher who is allowed to mistreat a child without being corrected by parents or the principal.
- *Being labeled and marginalized by a group as "different":* being poor, gay, part of an ethnic or religious minority, physically different, or following "a different drum."
- *Being cast out or sent away:* exiles, refugees, Native American children sent to government boarding schools, unwed mothers sent to "homes."

- *Being abandoned by primary caregivers when young:* orphans, children with a parent in jail, children being raised by extended family because their parents are addicts or alcoholics.
- *Chronic physical or emotional neglect:* dysfunctional parents can make children grow up to be shameful adults who feel they are not worth any positive self-regard.
- *Repeated failures in a public situation:* a child with an undiagnosed learning disorder failing in school.
- *Serial misfortune:* if people have enough bad luck events in a row, they may start to think there's something wrong with them.
- *Being blamed by others for their misfortune:* an unwanted child who is reminded by his or her mother that having a child ruined her chances for other things, the child of a stressed-out parent who is frequently shouted at for no reason, the person who receives blame for another's accidental death or injury.
- *The doctrine of original sin and the fall/redemption theology of the Catholic church:* there's nothing like being told you have something wrong with you from the moment you are born! Let's dump that fourth-century invention, shall we? Jesus would want us to.
- *Shame-based family systems:* such systems teach shame every day, repeatedly reinforcing the message, *You're no good! You don't deserve anything.* This can be said in words or carried implicitly in the attitudes and behaviors of the family.
- *Shame-based schools and institutions:* some rigid fundamentalist schools, some military units, some jails, the welfare system, the immigration deportation department.
- *The collective experience of being a conquered people:* Native Americans, African Americans, Irish, and other people around the world are still dealing with the footprint of shame in their groups, collectively.

Shame is a liar. Have you ever seen a "bad" infant? I haven't. We are each born pure and good, and our essences retain that innocence and purity inside, despite our bumpy journeys and all the "hits" our personalities have taken. Spirit still sees us as precious, innocent children who are mastering our developmental tasks. What if we looked at our own adult struggles with the same affectionate delight and encouragement with which we watch a precious toddler learning how to walk? Toddlers stagger forward, fall down over and over again, cry with frustration, and reach for a hug and a kind word. Then they get up and try it again and again, until it is mastered. Onward! To the next learning task! Our psychological and spiritual journeys are just like that. Spirit watches us with bemused encouragement, holding us blameless, and It reaches down to lift us up when we raise our arms in frustration and cry out. When we are sufficiently comforted and have released our stress, we toddle forward again.

How to heal your shame:

1. Decide it's OK to feel good about yourself.

2. Start to recognize the voice of shame as a liar.

3. Take a fierce stand against the voice of shame within: shout it down! Say a new truth.

4. Take a walk, go work out, punch a punching bag—expel the energy of shame with movement and vigorous positive thoughts (say them out loud, if you can).

5. Identify a few formative experiences in your earlier years that installed the energy of shame.

6. Heal, through forgiveness, each one of those formative experiences.

7. Do some inner child work and traumatic stress work if necessary.

8. Conduct a self-esteem campaign for a full year.

9. Work with a therapist or group to say your truths without shame and to practice revealing your real feelings.

Emptiness: healing the wound of the neglected heart

I want to take some time here to discuss a "self" problem for which many of us take the blame, even though it arises from circumstances that are not our fault. It is the wound of the neglected heart, which causes a feeling of emptiness inside. Sometimes, even when we are surrounded by people who care about us, we don't feel seen, understood, or loved. We lack the capacity for true happiness and fear that this is a self-inflicted negative attitude or some other character defect. Our fear worsens with our feelings of helplessness. This low-grade chronic loneliness usually has roots in a childhood where we seldom received generous, open attention from our parents.

Some of us grew up in an era when busy parents were glad if they managed to raise us with enough to eat and get us through school with a few practical skills and some decent values. If your parents gave you only what you needed to survive but not what you needed for your heart and spirit to *thrive*, then the ability to thrive may elude you as an adult. This is especially true in large families with a number of children; your parents may have missed the fact that you also needed individual time with them to be held, helped to solve a problem, or just spoken to with more awareness and kindness. Similar to a houseplant that thrives if it is given the proper light and watering for the type of plant that it is, a child needs affection for, and reflection about, who he is from those who are raising him, if he is to blossom. If you didn't get encouragement at a time when you were trying to "sprout" a new part of yourself and reach for the sun, that part of your individuality may have withered away, leaving behind it a baffling sense of loss that you can't consciously name.

If you recognize yourself here, consider forgiving your well-meaning parents for not providing you with nurturing attention. It wasn't their fault, either—most parents weren't expected to nurture the self-esteem of their kids and may not have received it from their own parents—but this "failure" on their part hurt you. There is a lost child inside you, frozen in a lonely and needy state since a certain developmental stage in your growing-up years. You wanted to experience more intimacy and affection with your parents. You craved a caring touch and loving praise for who you were as an individual. If this was missing from your childhood, even though your parents never once lifted a hand to harm you, you carry the long-held and silent wound of emotional neglect. You wear a gray cloak of mild depression around you that mutes your happiness, even in good times, because you are unconsciously grieving a loss. This loss was the chance to feel "special" to your parents and to yourself as you grew up. Your heart aches for the nourishing glow of simple self-love.

Forgiveness work can help heal this kind of depression. If you take some time now to forgive the lack of attention that you received as a child, a part of you will grow up happy at last. Use the Eight Steps to Freedom to address the key points in your childhood where you needed more nurturing and attention, *and that gap will become filled in now, in the present, by energy from your soul and the Universe.* With the help of a Higher Power—which can be seen as Mother or Father, if you wish—you can gracefully fill in some of the needed love and learning of previous developmental stages. You will walk taller, with the ordinary nobility of a healthy person. You will have a new ability to receive all the love that is already around you in the present. As you thoroughly address this wound of emotional neglect, your precious heart—cool and empty for so long—will become warm and contented at last.

"Falling Short" and Human Perfectionism

There is a nearly universal form of perfectionism hard-wired into human nature. It is the belief that we are "falling short" of what we should be. It is the habit of feeling somewhat disappointed in ourselves. We refuse to recognize and celebrate the success of our lives exactly as they are. Here's my theory about it: the *80% Rule of Purpose and Perfection.*

I came to the *80% Rule of Purpose and Perfection* one day when I was thrashing myself about my inadequacies. I usually have a clear mental vision of my goals and what it is I'm attempting to create in my life. It's perfect in my head, but the reality on the ground is so different than what I had hoped for. I often feel like a failure. Of course, part of the problem here is the *speed* and clarity with which the mind operates, and the *slowness* of the physical body and all of its attendant needs—like eating, sleeping, exercising, and making money for necessities. When I add in the time it takes for the maintenance of a few quality relationships, and the attention that goes to taking care of my house, my children, and my laundry, the day is just gone, long before I can take

my next four effective steps toward becoming rich and of great use
to the planet.

This was frustrating me like crazy, and one day I plunked
down in my favorite chair and wailed about what a failure I am.
I really believed I should have manifested some "big stuff" by
then. As usual, Spirit listened patiently for a while, awaiting the
chance to talk to me as soon as I settled down long enough to listen. When I reached the end of my whine, I breathed deeply for a
little while and cleared my mind completely. I cocked my head
quizzically, in the manner of a little dog trying to understand
something, and sincerely requested Spirit to "dish" on this topic.
This is what I heard:

*I know you are trying very hard to get everything just right and to
get a lot done, but what you need to know is that your own expectations of yourself are so much higher than mine. Nobody on Earth gets
to accomplish 100 percent of their plans, and nobody in Spirit expects
you to be able to do that. It's impossible! Plans just don't translate so
smoothly between Heaven and Earth, and I only expect you to succeed
at an approximation of what you planned to do before you came. In
fact, the most successful human beings never get any higher than 80
percent of their plans "right." If you aim for fulfilling 80 percent of
your goals and desires and get as close as you can to that, you will be
doing very well indeed, and I will be so pleased with you. Remember:
ultimately, it's all about love, anyway. Please let go of this human perfectionism that torments you. Achieve an approximation of what you
dream of accomplishing in your life on Earth, and be fine with it. It's
certainly fine with me.*

This is one of the many helpful messages that have come to
me over the years when I've brought myself to the conversation
with the Divine and the task of forgiving myself. In fact, during
the first few years of practicing forgiveness, I kept a journal in

which there was a section for the messages and insights that came out of my self-forgiveness exercises. Each time I reached the transpersonal point of view and forgave myself, I also taught myself something very important. I learned that I am always way too hard on myself, and that my harsh judgments and "failures" are really a human invention and not at all the way my Higher Self sees me. How does my Higher Self see me? How does yours see you? Our Higher Self sees us as perfect and whole, cherished children of the Universe, learning what we need to learn.

Steps of Self-Forgiveness

1. Prepare yourself: Sit on the floor or in a chair, and align your will to make a change. Decide to stop carrying this issue against yourself. Imagine your Higher Self above you, listening compassionately and waiting to grant you the relief of self-forgiveness. Use an image of an eternal field of light or another image of the Higher Power that works for you.

2. Talk out your problem in detail with your Higher Self like you would with a trusted friend or advisor. Ask It for help. Allow your full misery to surface and let your emotions out about it. Remember, there is nothing you can say or do that is unforgivable.

3. Connect with your Higher Self and lift yourself to Its level of consciousness. Lift above the emotional level by first see-ing the good in yourself and saying a few examples of that out loud. Visualize your image of your Higher Self again and meditate on some of Its qualities: light, peace, wisdom, generosity, compassion, and so on. Symbolically lift

yourself, as a soul, to the level of the Higher Self, leaving your personality down in the chair. Stand and turn to face your personality from above as you continue to fully resonate with God's great qualities. Allow your heart and mind to expand to the highest level and perspective: become pure light.

4. Grant yourself forgiveness from this higher level. As the Higher Self, in a state of love and light, look down upon where you were sitting and picture your personal self there awaiting your help. View your personality and his or her situation from a universal and expansive perspective. Extend your hands in healing and blessing, imagining light flowing through you and from you down into your personal self, releasing it from all burdens. Speak words of advice, wisdom, and comfort out loud to your personal self from this higher perspective. (Or just enjoy the silence and peace of the Self.) When you feel complete, make a definitive statement like, "I forgive you completely," or "I release you from your shame." (Note: If, during this communication in Step Four, you are expressing any judgment or criticism of your personal self, you are still in your personal self. Go higher, literally. Stand on a chair or a desk and try again. Your mind understands this physical metaphor and will cooperate.)

5. As your personal self, give thanks for the forgiveness and take in your new perspective. Return to your sitting position and quietly allow this experience to settle and integrate. Note the relief and new understanding. Say: "Thank you for this forgiveness."

5

Tackling the Big Ones

As I said at the beginning of this book, the process of forgiveness is exactly the same whether you are healing a minor annoyance or a tragic personal loss. Small to big, the steps and stages are there, helping you along to complete resolution. The Eight Steps to Freedom apply to forgiving things that are bigger than a single human being—for example: your government, your church, God, the Holocaust, an organization, your workplace, your family, women, men, slavery, a race of people, famine, broken treaties, war, genocide, terrorists, cancer, sexual abuse, alcoholism, evil, death, floods, hurricanes, earthquakes ... life!

Yes, sometimes you have to forgive a "Big One." The Eight Steps method is the same, in all of these cases. You can put something in the chair that symbolizes this larger thing and go for it! You'll find when you are done that this "big" thing has no further power over you.

One time, I found it necessary to forgive *life*—it had been one of those years. I was at a workshop with Edith in Chicago in 1988, and as we went around with introductions and goals on

Friday night, I tearfully dictated the laundry list of my recent losses: my late miscarriage, our bankrupt family business, the sudden closing of our wonderful daycare center, and my husband's injury and destroyed health. Edith smiled serenely and said, "Congratulations. You are being invited to go to a new level." (Oh, the things an adorable little lady with snow-white hair can get away with saying....) I decided to collapse all my issues into one, because I was most aware of my distressing inability to prevent losses in my life. With the help of another person, I chose to forgive *life*. We stood together at a big picture window that looked out over the city landscape under the night sky. I released my expectations that my family would still have all those valuable things that we had lost; that life would be smooth and predictable; and, of course, that everything would be within my control. I guess I did indeed go to a new level that weekend, because I came out of that experience with a newly minted lifelong commitment to live the life of unconditional forgiveness.

In this chapter, I will address a few of these "Big Ones": God, physical abuse, sexual abuse, and evil. I encourage you to do any or all of the following after you read this chapter: have a bracing cup of tea, take a walk in the fresh air to look at flowers and trees, pet your cat or dog, read a sweet and innocent tale to your child, rent a funny movie, and say your prayers at bedtime.

Forgiving God

"You know who I really need to forgive? *God!*" He spat out the word as though it were the name of a famous mass murderer or someone who had viciously attacked him. He was seething with anger, a fiery sheen of indignation that was thinly painted over his desolate loss. "I wasn't ever very religious, but when my daughter's mental illness got so bad it was life-threatening, I was willing to try anything. So I got into religion for a while, you know, really seriously. I joined a high-energy, upbeat Evangelical church, and I tried, I really *tried*. I prayed a lot; I kept my attitude totally positive; I believed every day that, with God's help, everything would be OK in the end. She committed suicide anyway. And now my son, who is also mentally ill, is saying suicidal things lately. I don't even want to talk to God."

Mike was an intelligent and likeable man I had just met at a dinner party. I nodded mutely, because sometimes there aren't any words that are the right words. My heart ached as I listened to him; I understood, a little. More than once in my life, I, too, have found it necessary to "break up" with God. The day after I met Mike, I found an email from him that included a poem he had just written. His poem, so emotionally honest, carried in it the feeling so many people have when they have experienced a tragic loss—completely bereft of faith and abandoned by the God they thought they knew. Mike told me he was aware that he was starting his process toward forgiving God, and as he put it, "You will see that I am turning the ignition to forgiveness—but the battery is very cold."

"How do you forgive God?" someone inevitably asks at our weekend forgiveness workshop. There most likely isn't someone named "God" who's sitting on a throne in Heaven getting it right or getting it wrong. Even the word "God," from its origin in the Teutonic word *Gheu*, means "to invoke," leaving us in a relationship with an open-ended mystery. The Eastern philosophical tradition of Taoism (as translated by Stephen Mitchell) puts it like this: "The Tao that can be told is not the eternal Tao. The name that can be named is not the eternal Name. The unnamable is the eternally real."

We do not have the power to make the great Self of the Universe abide by our human wills. What we always have the power to do is to willingly evolve what our *concept* of God is, setting aside an outmoded concept when necessary and questing again into a new level of understanding this mystery. Mike needed to forgive his concept of God: a concept he had signed up for when he'd joined the Evangelical church. That version of God was an all-knowing, concerned, and protective parent figure. This was a God who was supposed to answer prayers and prevent human tragedy. This God was supposed to help people and grant their wishes if they were good people who prayed a lot with unshakable faith, remaining very positive at all times. Yet this version of God had failed Mike. It had comforted and uplifted him for a while, but when it did not prevent his daughter's death, he felt betrayed and devastated. He had slammed the doors of his heart shut to God, but it was clearly hurting him now. Somehow he had to start finding his way out of his miserable, stubborn corner and start living again.

As I told Mike, I believe that if your concept of God has failed you—if you are closing down instead of opening up when things are hard—it's time to "fire" that particular version of God. Forgive it and send it packing. Then ask the Universe to show you a new concept that brings you forward—one that keeps you open and learning. Mike managed to do just that, and after a workshop and a private session, he is moving forward with his "new" God. He is still very sad about the tragic loss of his daughter, and he misses her, but he has managed to move beyond a state of blame about this tragedy. He has let go of his need to blame anyone for her death, including God.

Which religion, church, or spiritual practice offers us the best answers in the face of such tragedy? A teacher of mine once said,

"Religion is the car that you drive up to the house of God. But in the end, you have to get out of the car and walk inside to meet God on your own two feet." In the end, the best a church community can offer us is some company while we explore our big "God" questions for ourselves. It's wonderful when a church or spiritual belief system supports our personalities comfortably, like a well-fitting suit. It's nice to trust, to stretch out into our faith and deepen into it for a lifetime—what a treasure! But sometimes our faith classrooms only fit for a while, and then we outgrow them. If that's the case we must see where our souls lead us next, in an open-ended exploration as we search for a more meaningful spiritual practice. I don't think "God" has any problem with a person who has an eclectic approach—as long as the Love part is really happening.

I have chosen to please myself by worshipping the Divine Mother as my deity of choice. In my longtime relationship with Her, I've come to adopt the point of view that She is only peripherally interested in giving me the things I want and ask for in prayer. Nevertheless, I pray to Her often and ask Her for stuff, just like my own children ask me for treats and opportunities. *Sure, fine*, She says sometimes. *No, I don't think so* is the implied answer at other times. I'm not disappointed as often these days, because I realize that God never promised me that She would protect me from all the hard things that come along. Nor will I be allowed to keep my favorite people from harm, death, or their own problems. It's just not part of the deal here. From what evidence I do have, I think God, my Divine Mother, is very interested in supporting my learning experiences and my studies of universal laws: unconditional love, forgiveness, compassion, mercy, justice, humility, peacemaking, strength, trust in our resources, service, stewardship, the eternal present moment ... as my teacher in the School of

Life, She is all over the job of giving me what I need to learn every day. I feel Her expressing Herself within me as my own soul, a spark of a Higher Power, and as far as She's concerned, it's all about the learning. Sometimes I receive a few things along the way that are intended to appease my personality and my desires. (I love it when that happens.)

One day I watched my teacher Edith help a woman named Ann to forgive her concept of God. Ann was mad because she felt that God did not notice what she needed and did not care very much about her. This glum, hardworking young lady felt that she didn't matter to God or anyone; she worked and worked and tried to be good, and yet her own personal life was still empty and difficult, especially financially. She believed that God was there for others, and that He would certainly help them when they asked for help, but that He simply had no time for her. He never answered her prayers. She felt tired, overworked, and alone, and it seemed like everything she did was fruitless and led nowhere.

Sometimes people have a parent-child image of God, and their relationship with God mirrors the growing-up relationship they had with their own parents. Interestingly, Ann's concept of God was clearly a reflection of her relationship with her parents. She was a quiet child who worked hard at her chores and in school, yet she received little personal attention from her caring but busy parents. They always overlooked Ann's accomplishments and her needs because the bigger, louder personalities in her sibling group overshadowed her. If she felt unimportant and untended, no one ever noticed.

When Ann was done expressing her disappointment in her relationship with God, Edith guided her into an altered state of consciousness in which she invited Ann to "step into a new version of God." From this point of view, Edith told her to look at herself and her life situation and see what her "new God" wanted to show her. This is the vision she reported:

"I see myself digging a hole in the ground with a shovel, trying to reach the water table so I can have a well full of water, because I am thirsty. I am alone, bent over with the task, and my back hurts as I steadily dig and dig. Occasionally, I wipe away my tears, because I feel like I am getting nowhere; this is taking such a long time. I am tired and sad and I don't know if I will ever reach the underground water; I am afraid I will always be thirsty. What I can see from here, though, as I look through God's eyes at myself, is that right behind me, not far away, there is a waterfall! The fresh, clear water shimmers down, flowing and flowing, right nearby, and there is even a golden cup sitting on a rock at the foot of the waterfall, waiting for me to take a drink there. There is plenty of water, an abundance of it, if I would only look up from my work and receive what is already there for me."

Then and there, the energy in that transpersonal vision helped Ann to shed her disappointing concept of God. She suddenly realized that it was her own beliefs that had kept her life lean and empty; she had unconsciously taken on the image of a God who overlooked her needs, because of her position in her family. She decided to step completely outside of this concept and choose a new belief: *What I need is close at hand, and there's plenty for me.* From that day forward, her spiritual life was transformed—Ann experienced her new God as a steadily refreshing Presence, and she frequently reminded herself to look up and see the waterfall flowing nearby, and to reach for her cup whenever she needed water. Her experience these days is that her needs are always met by a generous, limitless Source.

Bill was mad at God too. He'd had a bad year in business and had found it necessary to work very hard for eighteen months so his business could survive the slide in the economy. A man of faith, he ran an ethical, service-based company that attempted to treat customers and employees with a lot of *heart*. Because of this, Bill felt that he should get some extra "points" with God, a serious break or two. After all, wasn't he working for God in the world, in his own way? But there were no breaks for him: only lots of trips, budget cuts, tough decisions, and a reduction in staff that he had to cover with his own time. On top of this situation, he had a new baby, and his wife needed a lot of support and help. Bill felt that he was already pushing a boulder uphill, and now he also had to help someone else climb the hill at the same time. It wasn't fair! Bill turned away from God for a while, but he brought his best to both his business and his family, one day at a time.

After this long, difficult stretch, things evened out and became stable again in Bill's business. His wife and baby reached a more comfortable stage and didn't need him as much as they had right after the birth. But he was still turned away from his God. For six months, he refused to pray or remember God throughout the day, as he had used to, but finally he realized that he didn't want to stay on the outs with God anymore. There was something missing in his life, something that used to enrich his day. One morning when he was in his office alone, he knelt down, looked up, and grumpily said, "OK, Lord—I'm letting you in again. But would you please tell me why you didn't give me more help? Why did it have to be so frickin' *hard?*" He closed his eyes and waited, and just like he used to hear it, the inner voice returned to him with some words of truth: *It was hard because you were in a strengthening process, and sometimes getting stronger hurts.* Bill had no argument for this, because it was true. He had grown very strong in the last eighteen months and was now fairly undaunted by his business challenges. Like someone who has been working out at the gym, he was toned and vigorous in both his family and his business life, and now in his renewed connection with his Higher Power.

How to forgive God:

1. Prepare yourself to find a different understanding of what God is. Talk to the Universe about it until you are ready.

2. Put two chairs out in front of you. Visualize an image of your former or current version of God occupying the space of the chair on the left.

3. Feel your feelings about this image of God. Say your feelings out loud to that being in the chair. You can cry, or express your anger or your opinions about what kind of a job God is doing. Be very honest, even if you know you aren't being logical or spiritual.

4. When you've explained all of your emotions, tell that version of God that you are through with it. Fire it from the job! Cut all ties between you. Let this former relationship go completely.

5. Breathe. Empty out. Open up the crown of your head, and feel yourself reaching out trustingly into the Universe for the gift of a workable new relationship with a Higher Power. Take your time with this.

6. Sincerely ask to be introduced to Spirit in a new form, in a new way. Visualize a field of white light occupying the chair on the right.

7. Try to sense what that light's predominant spiritual quality is: Is it compassion? Love? Joy? Peace? What is its nature? Feel the resonance of that quality and connect with it at your heart center. Invite the light to appear as a symbol or a representative figure, if that is appropriate for you.

8. Now, following a strand of connection from your heart to the light, and remaining in a meditative state, move over to sit in that chair, in the space of that light, and imagine that you can look back to see your personal self still sitting where you started. From the point of view of your new version of God, tell your personal self what it needs to know now on its spiritual journey, and tell it the best ways to remain connected to the new Higher Power. Give your personal self energy and advice from your position within the light.

9. Return to your original chair, take in this new perspective, and receive the good transpersonal energy coming from the light into your heart.

10. Seek a fresh relationship with your new version of "God" through the habits and practices that were recommended to you. Remember to continue to strengthen this new relationship with Spirit, and try to discover what it is teaching you now about life in the Universe.

Forgiving Abuse

I've been in "the forgiveness business" for over twenty-three years now, and as you can imagine, I've heard a lot of bad stories. It is presumptuous for me to declare, "I've heard it all," but sometimes I feel like saying that. During these years, I have been passionately enthralled by the story of human brokenness followed by an unimaginable resurrection of the spirit—and although, at this point, I've seen it thousands of times, it is still new to me. The most intense aspect of my life's work is helping people who are recovering from childhood abuse at the hands of their family members. It is still unbelievable to me that anyone can do some of the terrible things that they do to an innocent child—a child entrusted to them to treasure, nurture, and keep safe from harm.

I heard some of the worst stories each time I taught a forgiveness retreat at Hazelden Treatment Center, a world leader in the field of recovery from chemical dependency. It makes sense that the worst stories come from people in recovery, because studies show there is a very high correlation between untreated trauma and substance abuse. Dig just a little into the story of someone who started drinking at age thirteen, and you find it—the repressed anguish of emotional neglect and physical or sexual abuse—it is there like a burning, bleeding sore at the core of the person's heart and sense of self. And a person who has gone through an untreated traumatic stress scenario as an adult is also much more likely to start a phase of substance abuse than a person who hasn't.

I worked with recovering people at Hazelden's Renewal Center in Minnesota for sixteen years, leading several forgiveness retreats every year from 1992 to 2008. For the first five years, after each retreat was over, I spent some time privately crying my heart out about child abuse. It was an interesting exercise for me in the study of transpersonal psychology because, at those times, I learned to distinctly recognize both my transpersonal and my personal selves. Then, as now, whenever I worked as a facilitator of forgiveness, I operated from the transpersonal self: with a simple act of will, I stepped into that space and proceeded into the Eight Steps to Freedom. I was loving, peaceful, confident, and emotionally detached as I helped my clients to release their rage and heartbrokenness. I was solid as a rock, steady in my faith that they would emerge before long into a newly restored state of wholeness. As I sat there in the strength of my soul, I was always aware of the circle of invisible light and help from Spirit that is holding our process.

While clients spilled out the heartbreaking details of their abuse, my soul shrugged with neutral compassion, acknowledging: *I know. This stuff happens. That doesn't matter now. What matters now is transforming this story into new energy in the Present. Don't worry; they are going to make it out. Just keep going....* Meanwhile, my personal self, which I had relegated to the bleachers in the back of my mind, had her own reaction to the horrors of the stories. As I saw the devastated inner children inside the earnest, courageous adults before me, my personal self went crazy with indignation. So after each retreat was over, after the last hug and grateful good-bye, I closed the door to the training room and sat down with my assistant to release the impact of the stories I'd heard. I thought about each person, how good and lovely they were, and how sad and sorry I was that they had gone through such undeserved hell. I cried and cried, occasionally looking at my assistant, both of us shaking our heads in disbelief. After a while, there was no more to say. Those people were fine now—truly healed—and so there was no use dwelling any longer on those sad stories. The stories had been witnessed and ministered to in a sacred manner, and it was time for me to let them go, forgive them, and let those things be over, for good. After a while, my assistant and I said a closing prayer and packed up our stuff, and I went home to walk the dog and rent a funny movie.

I have been forever changed by the privilege of being the attending midwife at the rebirth of so many fine individuals, and a few of them stand out to me. They have taught me about the indomitable nature of the human spirit.

Carl's story

Appreciation and gratitude to Carl G. for allowing me to share his story.

I loved Carl from the minute I first saw him standing in the waiting room at my office building. I didn't know yet what he was there for, but I could feel something inside me click into place with a dedicated will to help him. Physically huge and imposing, dressed in impeccable and expensive business attire, he seemed to fill the whole room. I was sure he was impressive and/or intimidating in the worldly spheres in which he traveled. Yet the person I saw in that first moment was a sweet, sincere eight-year-old child peeking out at me through a man's eyes with a question: *Can you help me heal my heart, please? Yes, I silently answered him. I will. I don't know what your issue is yet, but I think the two of us can get you free, with Spirit's help. We must both be very brave and very patient.* Before long I learned that everything about Carl was *big*: big brain, big heart, big ego, big businesses, big vision, big intuition, big life in relationship to the Universe. His personal issues were complex, and his clever defenses had defied his previous attempts at therapy. I could feel him testing me hard throughout the first session, poking at me in sophisticated ways to see if I could be easily tricked or scared off. I had to concentrate to keep my ego from being triggered, relying instead on that stream of insight from the higher level that knows more than what my brain can infer. At the end of a lot of verbal downloading, he sat back and kind of dared me to know what to do next. I opened my mouth and said what Spirit knew to be true: *You were shattered by something long ago, and your parts are circling around your central self like satellites and moons around a planet. It's time to call all the parts back inside you and become one person. I think we can do that, if we work very closely with your intuition and mine. We must both be brave and patient, and we must not give up on this before a year passes.* With relief, he declared—not in so many words—that I had passed the test, and he was in.

Carl was motivated to change himself because, intuitively, he knew that he was heading for a heart attack if he could not release the chronic, boiling pressure inside him. He had accomplished a lot in his life as a bold entrepreneur, but he was driven in all of his endeavors by the fire and adrenaline of submerged rage—a fuel source that is unhealthy and unsustainable for the long term. He wanted to be motivated by love, creativity, and generosity instead. It soon became clear that what Carl needed to do most was to forgive his father. The middle son in a large family, Carl was a specific target for his father's physical rage from the time he was four until he was eleven. A few times each week, his father hunted Carl down to beat him until he was black and blue and nearly senseless, all the while screaming derisive things at his young son as he pounded on him. A few times, Carl was sure that his own father was actually going to kill him. Eventually, he grew too big to be pushed around and too clever to be caught by his father as often, and so the physical abuse ended. But there was never an end to the severe emotional abandonment. Carl's father did not ever give him anything positive of himself, father to son. Carl raised himself—an intelligent, sensitive, and bighearted boy, walking around in an isolation tank of lonely rejection that he learned to keep hidden. He fathered himself the best that he could, telling himself the things he needed to hear and setting out to show himself and the world that he was good enough. *Carl, the relentlessly impressive producer and contributor.*

Carl and I met weekly for the next nine months. We worked all around the issue of forgiving his father, never addressing it directly because he wasn't ready. It was like we were methodically spading a deep circle around the roots of a tough, dead bush, preparing to tug the whole thing out at once, taproot and all, when it was time. When it seemed like it was almost time, I gently asked Carl if he was ready to forgive his father. He looked around my office and said, "You know what? I can't even go there. If I really feel my emotions about my dad's abuse, I'm pretty sure I will break everything in this room. I'd hate to do that to your office." He could, too—I didn't doubt it. So we made a special arrangement for Carl's forgiveness work and went out to my country property, an isolated place of woods and fields where he could make a lot of noise and break things. I gave him permission to break anything in the woods that was dead already and to use his voice at full volume without holding back. Carl warned me that he needed to punch things, and I was not to worry about his hands in the process. This was a man's fight.

Now Carl was ready, and he went there. He plunged into the heart of his pain, and he let it out. He pictured his cruel father there with us and told the man everything he'd ever wanted to, without fear of getting hurt this time. He roared like a bull, shouted obscenities at the sky, and punched his fists into trees, over and over until his knuckles were skinned and bloody. He kicked and pushed dead trees to the ground, tore down overhead branches, and sobbed deeply. For over an hour, he ranged across the whole territory of his wound—from rage, terror, sorrow, loneliness, and confusion, to bleak despair. He expressed his frustrating lack of inner confidence, his bewilderment about his unfortunate fate, and his grief about all the mistakes and lost years that came on the heels of his damaged childhood. I stood at least ten feet away while he discharged his pain, fearful of a stray fist or flying branch, and respectful of his (*big!*) sacred space. I coached him along, the two of us finely in sync with each other because of the trust that had been built over the previous nine months. One by one, the Eight Steps unfolded, and, faithful as the rising sun, the miracle of forgiveness happened again. At the very end of the process, Carl was in a deep and private moment, in a semi-fetal position facedown in the grass in the middle of the sunny field. After his previous storm of verbal expression, the long silence that enveloped him was eerie. I was aware of the silence in the woods and the sky; it seemed to me that everything around us was patiently witnessing this moment. The silence was saturated with praise and compassion for Carl, and every leaf on the nearby trees was in tune with him at this moment, waiting. Tentatively, I crept closer and knelt down to whisper to him, "Carl? What's happening? How are you?"

He heaved a long, long breath and, still speaking to the ground, said thickly, "How am I? I am ... *one*." I knew what he meant. This healing had ended his fragmented spinning, forever. His orbiting parts had entered him and seamlessly integrated as one person. Without his former pain, Carl felt space and peace inside, at last.

Carl continued to have realizations about himself and his father for another two years. But they were gentle realizations, a steady succession of quiet aha moments that continued his integration and understanding of himself. He still moves forward with his daring entrepreneurial ventures, but as he'd hoped, his new fuel is love, creativity, and generosity. His new center of activity is his mission, a philanthropic project that gives struggling families the community support they need and gives at-risk children a safe harbor. He works at this with all his heart, and his heart is healthier than ever.

Meghan's story

Reader, be advised. This is a sad and shocking tale about an unspeakable incident in the life of a twelve-year-old girl. It has a triumphant ending, and she is better than all right now. I have chosen to go into some depth with this story, because it's an example of a forgiveness issue that makes you ask, "How do you ever forgive that?" Hopefully, the level of detail in this story answers that question for you. But you may or may not want to read this one—it's up to you.

In 1995, I began my work with Meghan, a lovely woman whose stable life had erupted into psychological chaos when a buried memory of being raped suddenly surfaced from her unconscious mind into her conscious awareness. With vivid, horrible recall that emerged in painful bits and pieces over a few weeks' time, she remembered the traumatic incident that had occurred in the autumn of her twelfth year. With this memory came severe physical symptoms, mental disequilibrium and disassociation, and sudden flashes of the impulse to commit suicide. She entered a painful and amazing journey of recovery and discovery that stretched out over a number of years as she diligently worked with the parts and pieces of this bad story, discovering all the ways it had shaped her and controlled her life from where it had dwelt in her unconscious for almost thirty years. Her story is one of the glory of an ordinary person who mastered her personal experience of an atrocity.

Meghan was a good, responsible girl—and a lonely girl. Reared to be "mother's little helper," she had her hands full as the oldest daughter of a family that was dealing with the consumptive insanity of alcoholism. Thin, tense, and eager to please, Meghan's need for attention and nurturing went largely unnoticed in her family life. Her father was pleasantly absent in his beer and his reading, and she only knew a harsh touch from her frequently exasperated mother. They moved to a new neighborhood when Meghan was in sixth grade, and she struggled socially. Her peers swiftly labeled her as a "weird kid," and she spent most of her time after school at home, helping out with the little kids, or drawing—intently copying pictures of happy, pretty ladies from the Ward's catalog. She wished for a few things—a yellow hair band, fishnet stockings, the next Beatles album—but her family's income didn't cover things like that, and her own allowance was too puny to buy much.

One autumn day when she was in seventh grade, her caring but tipsy father noticed she had a lot of time on her hands, and he recommended that she take a bike ride through the neighborhood to visit "Uncle" Pete, who was a trusted friend of his. So she and her brother did just that, each enjoying their own ice-cold sodas—a luxury!—and their uncle's kindly, undivided attention for half an hour. As they left his house, Uncle Pete unobtrusively took Meghan aside and quietly invited her to come back again next Thursday, *alone*. He said she would get to do something nice, and he would pay her ten dollars. "Don't tell anyone," he warned her. "This is just special between you and me, OK?" His eyes were caring and affectionate, and Meghan felt a leap of hope in her heart. The full attention of an adult in her life was like water for a thirsty person.

Ten dollars! That was a *lot* of money. She could buy all the things she had been wishing for and have some left to save. As she rode her bike through the crackling autumn leaves that next Thursday, she rode with her head held high and her heart singing a song of pleasant anticipation. No one had ever been this nice to her as an individual before, and it felt very good. Even the sunlight seemed like it was there just for her, carrying the promise of better days to come. Therefore, she could not understand what was happening when she parked her bike in Uncle Pete's yard, and something inside her cried out, *Don't go in there!* She ignored it.

Uncle Pete greeted her with a smile, and she smiled back, nervously. There was something different about his smile, something hard and wary. As she crossed the threshold of his house, her stomach did a flip-flop and she stopped dead for a second. *Get out of here! Get out of here now!* screamed the voice inside her. But Uncle Pete's hand clamped down on her shoulder in a firm grip as he said, "Come on upstairs." The hand on her shoulder felt like a large bird's claw. He smelled of smoke and alcohol—familiar smells, to be sure, but today they sickened her stomach. Meghan was growing afraid and wanted to leave, but she couldn't. She was hard-wired to obey her elders, and something in her knew she would not be allowed to go away. Up the creaking stairs they went, and Uncle Pete opened the door of the first bedroom and pushed her in ahead of him, none too gently. Meghan remembers:

They are waiting behind the door; there are three of them. Two of them look mean; one of them looks scared, like he wishes he wasn't there. I don't know what this is . . . things happen so fast I don't have any time to figure out what is happening . . . I find myself kneeling on the floor by the bed, facedown with my nose in the dirty gray sheets . . . something presses up against my bare bottom—I don't know what it is, but it's too big! He presses in, and my bottom and my insides rip open in an extremity of unbe-lievable pain—I turn my head to look at him, my mouth open in a silent shocked scream that cannot find a voice—his eyes are cold, hateful, cruel. He is wearing a leather jacket with high school letters on it. He wants to do this, because he has to let his hate out. . . . To get away from my pain and his hate, I'm no longer in my body, but looking down from the ceiling. From up there, I somehow know that I am not going to die, that I will live through this.

The boy is finished. I am half-conscious and, I think, half-dead. But it is not over yet. I surface into consciousness to realize that now I am lying facedown in the stale bed, and the next one is here to take his turn. I wish and wish to die all the way right now, but I can't. I cannot feel my bottom any-more, because I am overwhelmed with panic instead from the sensation of nearly being smothered. His weight crushes down on the back of my ribcage. He is big, and I can't breathe, and I can't get up. Irrationally, I wonder how Uncle Pete could allow his own niece to die of suffocation in his house and not do any-thing to stop it. How could this boy not notice that he is hurting me? Don't they care if I can breathe, or if I live or die? Aren't we family? My brain collapses into blackness, and I fly far, far away until the second boy is done.

The third one can't do it. He is scared and crying. So Uncle Pete helps me up and gets my pants back on me. He brushes away my tears and smoothes my hair, saying, "You were a good girl. You'll be fine. Here's your ten dollars. Remember, don't tell anyone." I force an obedient smile and nod, still crying and shak-ing uncontrollably from head to toe. As I leave his front yard, it occurs to me: I must be a very bad girl for something so bad to happen to me, and for my uncle to think it is all right. This life is just too hard. . . .

Meghan staggered home on her bike, dizzy, wobbly, and unable to sit down on the bicycle seat. She pulled over twice to throw up in the bushes. Somewhere along the way, she took the ten dollars out of her pocket and threw it in a pile of leaves, vowing never to make a lot of money if it was going to hurt so much. She crept into the garage and hid for a while, and then she ran upstairs unnoticed. As she lay on the top bunk of the bunk bed, Meghan clutched the railing hard, willing herself not to ram her head full speed into the wall in an attempt to smash her brains out. Suicide is wrong, she thought, and for sure you won't get into heaven if you do that.

Later, in the bathroom, she saw that she was a bloody mess. She hid all of this from her mother, who was trying to cope with her toddler brother's latest head bump, a concerning one. Meghan perceived that her mother would not be able to handle this. Her mother noticed vaguely that Meghan was acting strangely, but then became distracted by someone else who needed her and forgot to notice Meghan again. Meghan did not tell her father about Uncle Pete hurting her, either. He would have found it preposterous, and she didn't even know how to say what had happened to her. She didn't know the word rape. It was 1967, a few years before the women's movement and a dozen years before the issue of sexual abuse blew wide open in society's awareness.

The next day in school, Meghan was still very disassociated— her consciousness disconnected from her physical body—and she felt like she was still hovering near the ceiling, uninvolved with anything going on in class. She had an accident in her pants, to the shock and disgust of the seventh grade teacher, and this sealed her fate as a hopeless weird kid in her class until graduation. The teacher had forty kids in the room, so he did not think to call Meghan's home and say, "Did something happen to Meghan?

There's something very wrong with her today...." He, too, had not yet heard the phrase *sexual abuse*. Gradually, Meghan's body healed, but her trauma was sealed in. She swiftly and completely *forgot* this unbearable injury, almost right after it happened. Her brain simply did not know what to do with it or how to categorize it. There was no "next step" to take for a healing process. So for many years, this memory was blacked out by her brain's survival mechanism, so she could go forward.

Meghan became jumpy, paranoid, and afraid to walk through doorways into unfamiliar rooms. She developed a deep sense of shame and blamed herself for anything that went wrong. As an adult, Meghan was unable to earn money unless it was a very small amount, when in reality she needed more money and was frustrated by her own baffling resistance to making it happen. She was still privately obsessed with a fear of having a public accident in her pants. She did not trust men and so, until her remarkable husband came along, she only had relationships with men whom she could completely control. Hypervigilant and controlling, she worried needlessly about her safety and, when she became a mother, she fretted about the safety of her daughters. She suffered from bouts of depression and lower back pain. Worst of all, she was most afraid when life was good. Whenever the feeling of pleasant anticipation about a future opportunity arose within her, she froze in terror and pulled back abruptly from the impending success and goodness. *It's a trick*, she would think. *I'm not going to trust it.* So she lived her life small, smaller than her generous spirit wanted her to, and even when things were good, she worried there would soon be a bad trick to take it all away. She believed, and thus experienced, *Life is too hard....*

Meghan was forty when her memory surfaced, and she sought out the best healing resources. She had created a life with a reasonable amount of blessing in it (if not very much money). Chief among her blessings was her gentle and sensitive husband, who deeply understood her and was helping her to trust people again. She was also well supported by friends in her spiritual community. She worked as a therapist, and she was a good one. Sensitive and compassionate, she had a strong commitment to help each client put an end to his or her suffering. And now she was determined to do that for herself, with her worst story. She wanted to talk to me about forgiveness because her spiritual instincts informed her that, ultimately, she had to forgive this atrocity if she was to be free. She knew that the power of this buried memory had been the source of all her baffling inner demons, and it had kept her afraid, financially limited, and living too small. We both knew it would be awhile, but we agreed that I would help her to forgive her uncle and the boys when she was ready.

Her journey of self-healing took her to many different places and through different stages. For the first two years, she saw another therapist and did some trauma release therapy, eye movement desensitizing and reprocessing, and sensory motor integration. She received hands-on healing energy and bodywork, and even some myofascial release on the scar tissue in her bottom, which improved her lower back pain. Her path led her to an appointment with a shaman, who restored to her some of her own energy that had been lost when she was a girl. He also extracted some ugly, hateful energy from behind her liver. He said it looked to him like a big black snake. The moment he took that energy out of her, Meghan said, "It's like the light went on, or the sun came out from behind a cloud, inside my brain. The long-term fog of depression lifted from my brain chemistry, and it stayed gone."

In addition to these alternative healing modalities, the Universe brought healing to Meghan in some surprising ways. In her therapy practice, she found herself working sequentially with two male clients who were tormented by memories of being roped into participating in gang rape by other males when they were younger. They suffered enormous shame and self-loathing, and one of them was practically paralyzed with depression. Like Meghan, he felt that he had lost something precious—his own innocence and sense of being "good." He, too, felt that he had lost himself to something he didn't understand. To her surprise, Meghan found that her native compassion and her ability to tap into a higher spiritual level came to her aid in helping these men to heal, and this work with them was healing for her too.

Another surprising healing event was the unanticipated support from Meghan's elderly mother. One late night while Meghan was visiting her mom, an intimate moment arose, and Meghan felt it was natural to share with her mother what had happened. Hardly believing she was really doing it, Meghan found herself sharing her sad secret at last. Her mother declared, "Somehow, I'm not surprised by this. I believe you completely." Tearfully, Meghan poured out her private, awful story in every detail, and then her mother held her as they cried together for the injured twelve-year-old girl. Her mother apologized for having been too stressed and self-absorbed to realize that something was wrong, and she affirmed Meghan's decision not to tell her at the time. "It's true," she said. "I couldn't have handled that at all. It would have sent me over the edge. You were smart not to tell me." Meghan leaned into her mom's shoulder while her mother's wrinkled hands stroked her hair. Together, they constructed a healing fantasy, rewriting the story to match what they wish had occurred. As Meghan tells it:

We imagined that I went home after being gang raped and immediately told my parents what Uncle Pete and those boys had done to me. My parents dropped everything and took me to the hospital to receive medical care, and we filed a police report. Uncle Pete spent many years in jail. My parents took me to therapy and healers for a long time until I was well recovered. I left my grade school and finished my education through eighth grade with a talented and insightful tutor. The two boys were ordered into a program for young sexual offenders, and they got therapy too. We let our family and friends in on the story, and no one blamed me for this terrible thing. I entered high school in the spirit of a "fresh start," which included a close and trusting relationship with both of my parents, who were now sane and healthy, ever mindful of how I was doing. I trusted life and was open to goodness and blessings, as I still am to this day.

That night Meghan's dreams were filled with the sound of joyous trumpet music and the spirit of freedom and celebration. A Being of Light was with her in her dream, as she danced with abandon.

Several years after Meghan had stated her intention to forgive the perpetrators of her rape, she felt ready to work with me and do the Eight Steps to Freedom. She forgave her "uncle" first, and in another session much later on, she forgave the boys. Forgiving Uncle Pete took almost three hours, and in Step Two (Express Your Feelings), Meghan was amazed at how much grief and rage were still inside her, bucketing out in torrents. She enjoyed the fantasy of viciously pushing Uncle Pete's old body down a long flight of cement stairs and following him down there to kick him to death. We put cushions on the floor to represent him, and she kicked them over and over many times before she was ready to move on to Step Three (Releasing Your Expectations). She released the expectations that Uncle Pete would have been as trustworthy as he first seemed, that she really could have done something nice with him, and that he would have given her clean money earned by honorable actions. She released her expectation that an uncle is always a man who nurtures, honors, and protects his niece, keeping her from harm if he is around. She released her expectation that Uncle Pete and the boys would have been healthy people, and that she herself could have known to avoid a situation like this completely. And she released the expectation that her life after age twelve would have proceeded in a healthy way, with trust and optimism for her pathways to opportunity.

At a certain point in the spiritual stages of this forgiveness work, Meghan was in a very altered state and spoke of her new understanding and awareness of the moments her soul hovered near the ceiling of the room while her body was being raped. With the pain behind her now, she gained a valuable new perception of all that was going on in those few moments.

From above, I saw that there was so much pain in that house—I didn't know there was so much pain there. I didn't know pain could make someone do this to someone else. From above the situation, I felt compassion for them, even though I was witnessing this terrible action being done to my person. Also, I had a sense of a Being of Light there with me; it bathed the scene with light and held me in its strength and compassion while this action unfolded. It protected me from becoming shattered beyond repair. It reminded me that I was not going to die from this. Somehow, I have the feeling that this event was always meant to happen; somehow, it's part of what I'm here for—part of my purpose here.

When she was through all of the Eight Steps to Freedom, Meghan was emotionally spent but strong and resolved inside. She had nothing left except for a feeling of compassion for Uncle Pete and the boys. This honest compassion toward her attackers is something that is hard for many of us to comprehend. Her pain was gone, and there was a new space inside her that permitted her to step back and look at the wider landscape.

As a therapist, Meghan was familiar with the fact that most sexual abuse perpetrators are also people who experienced sexual abuse when they were young. Very often they do not remember it until they are in trouble for doing the same sort of thing to someone else. One would hope that people who had an awful experience like that wouldn't want to cause the same kind of distress for another person. But, for some reason, it doesn't work that way with the issue of sexual abuse. Often, a victimized person shoves that experience deep into his or her unconscious mind, where it lives in the dark, split off from the person's awareness, conscience, and self-concept. Like a poisonous snake living in a jar with a lid, it bides its time, waiting to come out and express itself. It is an aggressive creature spawned from the human delusion that if one is frustrated and empty of natural power, one can take power from a person who is more vulnerable. Meghan was aware that Uncle Pete had grown up in an orphanage, and it was quite possible that he, too, had been the victim of this kind of abuse.

Meghan mused and theorized, and filled out the story in a way that made a little sense out of something senseless. In the end, she'll never know how or why one person can do something so wrong to another person. What she does know is that this experience shaped her path like nothing else in her life, and now she has to be at peace with it.

She moved on. She let the story go, for long periods of time. Periodically, another facet of this event presented itself for healing. When it did, she tended to it for a few weeks, until it melted away again into new insight, new strength, and wisdom. She knows now that evil is a real factor in human existence. I enjoy watching Meghan move through the world with more openness and ease in her body these days. She always trusts her fine-tuned intuition without hesitation. Her reputation as a talented therapist has grown, and she allows herself to enjoy more prosperity. Her success is due in part to the way she is a fierce advocate and an understanding counselor for the victims of sexual abuse who show up in her practice. She can even work with clients on either end of the abuse cycle—victim and perpetrator—seeing them as equally wounded by their participation in an atrocity.

I asked her if she thought she could completely get over a story like this. Meghan said:

> Probably not 100 percent. Because of this event in my life, I now know from personal experience that even good human beings do horrible things sometimes, and they do them to innocent children. That is wrong, and though I am mostly over my own story, I will never stop caring about this issue, for all of us. Until this kind of story vanishes from our world, for everyone, I will not be completely free of it either. Because of my story, I have become part of the effort to end abuse and its effects. I will probably always have a phantom streak of paranoia, but I'm OK with it. I talk to it and laugh at myself when I'm being crazy. It's like my life now is a big, beautiful garden with one ugly little bit of debris in it that can't be removed for this lifetime. I have to accept that it is there and enjoy the garden anyway. I am becom-

ing an innocent again, because I want to trust Life. But it's an "informed innocence" from now on.

To me, Meghan looks perfect and wonderful—a walking miracle and a living reminder of the freedom of forgiveness and the restorative forces of the Divine Feminine in this world. Soft as rain, strong as steel, and pretty as a flower, Meghan is gently indomitable in her ultimate faith in humanity. She lives and works as a healer with the ease and dignity of a master. Her wound has indeed become her wisdom.

Forgiving Evil

"How could anyone ever do something that evil?" Time and again, we hear that anguished question bursting out of someone after a story about a senseless and brutal act like the one that Meghan suffered through. This question frequently arises in the forgiveness workshop when we are exploring the idea that you can forgive *everything*. People are baffled by the quality of evil inside certain stories and wonder if it is even *right* to forgive those things. As a father of murdered children put it, five years after his loss: "I'm not going to forgive this. I think God wants us to hate evil." However, I appreciate the words of Lewis B. Smedes about this: "When we forgive evil we do not excuse it, we do not tolerate it ... We look the evil full in the face, call it what it is, let its horror shock and stun and enrage us, and only then do we forgive it." I agree with that approach.

No one knows for sure what causes people to do evil things. Is it a matter of terrible alienation from self and society, or other errant psychological forces inside them? Is there an actual force of evil in the Universe that possesses certain people—a larger spirit of evil that is the real driver of these inhuman actions? We don't know, and ultimately, that's not what matters. What does matter is that if you ever are in the rare and unfortunate situation that requires you to forgive something that is evil, you can do that successfully. You can free yourself even from these baffling, awful things and become strong and whole again. When you are ready to forgive an atrocity and take your situation through the Eight Steps to Freedom, you will have peace and relief—I promise! I have seen this many times.

6

In Harmony with the Universe

I used to do everything the hard way. If it was possible to do something with much more worry and struggle than was necessary, I found the way to do it. I braved my life alone, burdened with stress, responsibility, and a perfectionist's chronic unrest. I was like the sad, moody person in the whimsical quote by William Butler Yeats: "Being Irish, he had an abiding sense of tragedy which sustained him through temporary periods of joy." The only comforting thing about living like this was the lofty idea that I was a brave soldier in the front lines of a battle for good and justice in the Universe. If it was a lonely and trying existence, at least I could pride myself on being some kind of hero. Then one day I was introduced to a different way of living. Like a soft spring breeze blowing on my strained forehead, something new entered my life—something called *grace*. I'd heard about grace all through the years of my religious upbringing, but I had no idea what the priests were talking about. I thought it was some kind of abstract but necessary currency that you earned with good behavior and faithful participation in church sacraments. But that's not it, after all.

The Stream of Life

I've come to think about grace as the palpable feeling of being at ease and in harmony with the Universe. We have modern words for it: *in the zone, you've got your groove, you've got it going on,* and *it's all good.* This kind of peace is not a static state, and neither is it a driven one. It is that experience of being in the *flow*—like a skilled canoeist in a smooth river, using the paddles lightly from time to time to steer back into the center of the current. The Stream of Life carries him along on its ample back, and at times, the journey is uneventful and serene, soothing his restless mind into spacious silence, into trust. At other times, the landscape changes and rapids approach. Danger is near. Yet the traveler remains relaxed and attentive, working with the elements and utilizing his strength and knowledge—this is peace in action. This is what living the path of Unconditional Forgiveness is like.

During the course of experiencing and witnessing so many healings, and having a sense of the healing energy that is always on tap for us, I have come to believe that there is a living stream of love and energy that extends itself to us from the origins of the Universe, from the heart of the Creator. This gift of light, creativity, and blessing freely offers itself to everything and nourishes every living creature. It softly sings to us a wordless song, yet if our human minds could put words to it, they might be the tender words of a Mother: *Thrive, dear one, thrive. I want the best for you, and look! Right here—I've brought you just what you need now. Receive it, please. I love you so. . . .*

Like canoeing well through the rapids of a river, or any task requiring some skill, you learn how to live in harmony with the Universe from other people who have mastered it. In Eastern understanding, you learn through your relationship with the guru. The word *guru*, or "darkness/light," is often misunderstood in the West. It refers to the formless force of teaching and illumination that kindles your awakening and brings you out of darkness into light. It usually manifests as another human being who inspires you and models wholeness for you, like your wise grandma; your serene AA sponsor; or a spiritual master, like Jesus. But perhaps you experience it in the resolute and life-affirming stance of your favorite tree or rock—ancient and knowing. This person or being opens the window in the unlit room of your small and difficult life. The guru lets the light in and shows you the vista that opens out to the flowering fields of the Universe.

For me, the guru took the form of my mentor Edith, appearing like a white-haired old woman in a pink suit; grace was this lady with a gentle smile and a sheen of white light around her as she did ordinary tasks with extraordinary simplicity and *presence*. After Edith, my guru took the form of the astounding synchronicity and uncanny uplift of everyone in the room each and every time I taught the forgiveness workshop. Again and again, my clients healed, I healed, and the healing began to spill over into my daily life with absurd persistence. I felt pursued by goodness, sometimes outright ambushed by love. This is just the sort of thing that is hard for a brave little soldier to take, but I finally had to give up and just let it happen. Forgiveness made my life easier and gave to me a new life metaphor. No longer am I a brave little soldier struggling in the trenches of a battlefield. I am a retired soldier now, a happy gardener in peacetime.

The Ripple Effect of Unconditional Forgiveness

As I began to travel outward around the United States and to other countries with my sturdy forgiveness workshop, this grace—this Universal harmony—met me in the early morning light as I rolled my suitcase out of my front gate. It was there in the brotherly eyes of the Somali cab driver who took me to the airport. It stood to serve me at the desk of the hotel where I stayed, and it stepped forward with a smiling hug from someone who brought me to her city to teach forgiveness—the new friend I hadn't met yet.

In every place I visit to teach the forgiveness workshop, stories of harmony with the Universe spring into being. These new stories drift back to me later, marvelous little wonder tales about the ripple effect of forgiveness in a family or a community: "and that very evening after your public talk, with no explanation, Grandma started speaking to her daughter again, after five years of bitter silence. . . ." From the stories I have heard, it appears that it only takes one person with forgiveness-inspired energy and goodwill to catalyze a new attitude of forgiveness in the family or community. Unconditional love travels out beyond the individual like ripples of water in a pond, quietly influencing everyone else in the person's sphere, and those people influence others. You can see this in your mind's eye: as you live the path of unconditional forgiveness and practice the Eight Steps to Freedom on this thing and that, more and more positive effects ripple outward . . . into your marriage, your family, your community, your city, your nation, and humanity as a whole.

What if more people on the planet took care of their personal pain, forgave everyone and everything, and actively strove to live in harmony with the Universe? What if we could end war and deprivation because a critical number of humans uproot our violent tendencies and replace our toxic energy with goodwill toward all? If the practice of unconditional forgiveness becomes widespread, perhaps humanity as a whole can heal itself, synthesize its disparate parts, and indeed discover its own soul. Each one of us contributes to the fulfillment of this possibility when we are committed to unconditional forgiveness. The transformative energy that shines out of a loving, soulful person who is living and working in harmony with the Universe cannot be overestimated!

A Child Comes Running Home

"It's not too late yet to have a happy childhood," Edith said once. Like a Zen master delivering a koan to her student, she had a straightforward way of occasionally saying things like that and then moving on to something else without explaining to me what she meant. Over the years, as I did forgiveness work for myself and others, I came to experience and understand it. As I shed layer after layer of the darkness created by the sporadic distressing events in my own childhood, I could instead remember what was good. Each session of forgiveness was like drinking a memory potion—suddenly I remembered good childhood memories that the bad ones had hidden. Like finding a lost photo album, I discovered forgotten memories of a happy childhood: there was the special birthday moment with my father, the blissful sunny day playing by the creek with my brothers, and the warmth of an intimate moment with my mother when we were both moved by something we saw. These ordinary sweet moments, long forgotten, are now in a treasure box inside my mind with a handful of other jewellike moments of intimacy with my family. Good memories slipped into place and wove together a new story, blending with the difficult moments into the tapestry of my life. The dark patches outline and show the shapes of the light ones. Even in a difficult childhood, there is so much that is good to remember and claim as yours.

I am amazed at the energy and the indestructibility of the happy, vibrant child inside each of us. He or she is just waiting for the chance to come out and play again, after being put aside for so long. A few times, I've been astounded at the sudden blast of physical vitality that bursts forth from the serious, tired adult I've just been assisting in a forgiveness workshop:

Kathy was tense and wired, with a tight jaw and neck muscles showing like taut cords because of the unrelenting stress of dealing with her abusive sister all her life. After Kathy forgave her sister, suddenly, there she was—the irrepressible six-year-old who had taken to hiding long ago because life wasn't very safe. Bouncing and exuberant, Kathy asked all of us to make some room for her, because she just *had* to do a cartwheel.

Marie cried about her mother's lack of affection and support for so long, I thought there would be no end to it. But as always, there was. Ever serious and striving to get everything just right, it was almost weird to hear the free-spirited little giggle that began to emerge from her as I debriefed her at the end of the Eight Steps. When I asked her what she wanted to do now and in her future, her eyes shone, and she said, "I want to play! Will you do leapfrog with me?" (*I'm forty-five*, I thought to myself. *Leapfrog requires young knees, doesn't it?*) Nevertheless, the group good-naturedly made room for us, and Marie and I leapfrogged together around the room for a few minutes while everyone laughed and clapped. At the end, Marie was invigorated and full of buoyant energy—ready for tomorrow.

Sandy had been hiding her true self for so long, caught in shame from being repeatedly sexually molested by her grandfather when she was a girl. Now in her mid-fifties, this lady was no fun, and she knew it. Grim and stodgy in her body language, and both physically and energetically heavy, she was bound up with criticism toward herself and others. When she forgave her grandfather and herself, releasing her harsh judgment toward both of them, it was like a dark cloud lifted out of the room and the sun came out. Sandy felt like she lost a hundred pounds, and she said that she felt so light she really believed she might be able to fly. She satisfied herself instead by stumping with determination up the long grassy hill outside Hazelden's Renewal Center. At the crest of the hill, she stopped to wave at her witnesses and lifted her arms joyfully to the sky. Then, very deliberately, she lay down on the ground and rolled all the way back down the hill.

Peggy was caught inside a rigid and barely penetrable shell of shame that had crippled her since she was five, when she accidentally spilled a pot of boiling water on her sister. She became the focus of the whole family's pattern of blame-and-shame, and it led her onto a miserable path of alcoholism and abusive relationships. She worked hard in recovery, but had difficulty with the assignment to stop beating herself up. I worked with Peggy at a treatment center in Ireland, and she did a powerful piece of forgiveness work in which she forgave her family system for making her the scapegoat and depriving her of love. Afterward, she was limp as a noodle, so we sent her to a quiet room with a friend to be with her while she integrated the experience.

Later that day she emerged, and her whole posture and way of interacting with us had gone through a transformation. With her head high, and her shoulders straight and strong, she looked us in the eyes and spoke with animation and abandon. *This can't be real*, I thought to myself. But I saw her again later in the week, and all evidence pointed to a real and lasting change. At the end of this second session, she pumped my hand in a vigorous hand-shake and said into my face with gusto, "Thank you very much, Mary. And now I will be *free!*" I shook my head in disbelief as I watched her hustle briskly away from me, across the sunlit lawn. Could this be real? Yes ... it was unmistakable. She was *skipping*.

Conclusion

As I complete this book and reflect on twenty-five years of my commitment to the path of unconditional forgiveness and the Eight Steps to Freedom, I can't claim sainthood or full enlightenment. What is true now is that I wake up most days in a state of pleasant anticipation, glad to be here. Life is good—difficult at times, but good. Everything I need is in front of me or right next to me. I can't blame anyone, including myself, for the things I don't prefer. It's enough in a day to do the next right thing, and if I don't know what that is, I pay attention to my breathing and whatever beauty is available until the next right thing shows up. It usually comes as an opportunity to share some kindness or loyalty with another human being. There is no need for unnecessary drama, because everyday life is glorious, ordinary, and gritty enough on its own. The part of me that was a frightened child is nestled safely at home in my heart— well loved, well tended, and well guided moment by moment. No matter how ordinary, noisy, and intense my current scene is, God's presence is knit into it and wrapped all around it like a cushion of unconditional love and quietude.

As Edith said to me once from the mountaintop of all her life experiences, "We don't know why they did that, dear.... In fact, dear, *we don't know anything at all.*" The peaceful twinkle with which that wise woman spoke that one sentence taught me more than anything else she said during our years together. She showed me that wisdom comes when you realize that, even if you don't know anything for sure, life is fine. Even if you don't know what is going to happen in the next moment, you are safe and whole, at home in the Universe. When you walk out into the day and, as Rumi said, "be a lamp, or a lifeboat, or a ladder" and know that whatever life presents you, you will find the good in it, you have received the full gift of living the path of unconditional forgiveness.

> *I thank Thee O Heavenly Spirit*
> *Because Thou hast put me*
> *At a source of running streams,*
> *At a living spring in a land of drought,*
> *Watering an eternal garden of wonders,*
> *The Tree of Life, mystery of mysteries,*
> *Growing everlasting branches for eternal planting*
> *To sink their roots into The Stream of Life*
> *From an eternal Source.*
>
> —FROM THE THANKSGIVING PSALMS
> OF THE DEAD SEA SCROLLS, VI (III, 19–36)

Appendix A

The Midwest Institute for Forgiveness Training Programs

Mary Hayes Grieco and the teaching staff of The Midwest Institute for Forgiveness Training are available to teach Unconditional Forgiveness in your community. Call our office toll free at 877-377-6232 or visit us at www.forgivenesstraining.com for our current schedule in Minneapolis/St. Paul, Minnesota.

Programs

The Forgiveness Weekend Intensive: The healing workshop that is open to the public, it is held four times a year in St. Paul, MN. Lecture, large group discussion, small group, journaling, meditation, demonstration, Eight Steps to Freedom (forgiving another), self-forgiveness. Eleven Continuing Education Units (CEUs). (*This intensive is not appropriate for people dealing with active addiction, emotional instability, or personality disorders.*)

The Freedom of Forgiveness for Mental Health Professionals: A one-day training program with an introduction to current research about forgiveness and health, and to the model and method of the

Eight Steps to Freedom. Includes a demonstration of the method with a volunteer, one experiential meditation exercise, and a discussion on applications of the Eight Steps method in clinical practice. Recommended for psychologists, social workers, clergy, CD counselors, marriage and family therapists, and nurses. Six CEUs.

The Nine-Month Self-Mastery Program: Nine weekends of spiritual teaching, holistic self-healing, and one-to-one mentoring with Mary Hayes Grieco. In-depth study of foundations of Unconditional Forgiveness: The Eight Steps to Freedom, psychosynthesis, subpersonalities, universal spiritual laws, intuition, subtle energy body, self-forgiveness, and life purpose. Twelve students accepted, by application and interview. Forty-two CEUs.

Customized Programs: Evening lectures; keynote speeches; minitrainings for treatment centers, hospitals, businesses, and churches.

Institute Staff:

Director and Lead Trainer: Mary Hayes Grieco
Public Workshop Teaching Teams:
Mary Flood-Maneely & Kiersten Dahl-Shetka
Teesie Vallero, Sue Paisley, & Dr. Kate Pfaffinger, PhD, LP
Professional Training Team:
Mary Hayes Grieco and one of the following:
Dr. Kate Pfaffinger, PhD, LP
Mary Conner, MA, LP
Dr. Todd Anderson, PsyD
Linda LaBarre, MA

877-377-6232, www.forgivenesstraining.com

Appendix B

Notes on Psychosynthesis and Transpersonal Psychology

Unconditional Forgiveness has its foundations in *psychosynthesis*, the life's work of Italian psychiatrist Dr. Roberto Assagioli (1888–1974). Dr. Edith Stauffer studied with Dr. Assagioli for several years near the end of his life, and she was tremendously influenced by his comprehensive model of transpersonal psychology.

Transpersonal psychology is concerned with the study of humanity's highest potential, and with the recognition, under-standing, and realization of unitive, spiritual, and transcendent states of consciousness. It attempts to describe and integrate spiritual experience with modern psychological theory, and to formulate a new theory to encompass such experiences. The pioneers who laid the groundwork for this field earlier in the last century include William James, Carl Jung, Abraham Maslow, and Roberto Assagioli. More recent contributors include Ken Wilbur, Jean Houston, Stanislav Grof, and Robert Sardello, among others. Dr. Assagioli's many colleagues and students appreciated him both for his brilliance as a theorist in the rapidly developing field of psychology, and for his steady, soul-illumined personality. As

Edith described him, "His eyes always twinkled with humor, kindness, and joy."

Dr. Assagioli referred to psychosynthesis as "the psychology of the soul." When his colleagues in the field asked him why he presumed to put the soul into the science of psychology instead of leaving it in the hands of the churches, he replied: "I did not put it in. I never took it out in the first place." His model hypothesizes that we exist on two levels, soul and personality, and that the job of psychology is to strengthen, heal, and clarify the personality, so that the light of the soul can shine forth into the world. This model lays out a path of self-development in which we, as healthy human beings, first master the tasks of each of our developmental stages, the building blocks from infancy to early maturity: infancy, toddlerhood, school age, puberty, and so on. Then, as mature adults, we consciously conduct a *synthesis* (or "bringing together") of our various parts into a working whole. First, we harmonize the different components of the personality—body, emotions, and mind—and we heal and organize our various "subpersonalities" under the directives of the central basic self, in support of its goals and purposes (see "Further Reading Resources on Psychosynthesis" below for more information about subpersonalities).

Once the personality is integrated, we synthesize it with the life and energy of the soul, or Higher Self, achieving a high state of awareness and functioning—the state that Dr. Abraham Maslow referred to as "self-actualization." As this union takes place, we become aware of our desires for true service to society, which is also in a process of an evolutionary awakening. This leads us into greater synthesis as we gain an even wider sensibility of ourselves as citizens of humanity and the Universe.

In 1938, Benito Mussolini's Fascist government arrested and imprisoned Dr. Assagioli because of his Jewish heritage and his humanistic writing. He was in solitary confinement for over a month; during this period, he spent much time in meditation and study, developing his spiritual psychology. After his release and his return to his family, Dr. Assagioli endured more losses and ravages of war, but he reentered his interrupted professional projects with joy and vigor as soon as the war was over. In addition to being a widely respected theorist in the twentieth-century milieu of Western psychology, he was a long-term student of Eastern mysticism. Long before yoga meditation made it into popular awareness in the 1960s, Dr. Assagioli and a group of colleagues were making their own experiential investigations as students of a Tibetan meditation master. Though he never named it as such, it is easy to see that his model and his book *Psychosynthesis* are blends of Eastern wisdom and Western psychology. Dr. Assagioli also had a passionate interest in the life and development of the will, and his book *The Act of Will* thoroughly explores this topic from different facets: the levels of will, the stages of willing, and the development of the will.

Each of Dr. Assagioli's works is a sophisticated tome delivering a visionary message about humanity's ultimate potential. Since Dr. Assagioli's death in 1974, hundreds of individual practitioners around the world have continued to develop psychosynthesis theory and practice. See the resources below for more information about Dr. Assagioli's life and work, as well as other articles, books, and papers written by today's students and teachers of psychosynthesis.

Further Reading Resources on Psychosynthesis

Roberto Assagioli, *Psychosynthesis: A Collection of Basic Writings* (Amherst: The Synthesis Center, 2000).

Roberto Assagioli, *The Act of Will* (Amherst: The Synthesis Center, 2010).

Pierro Ferrucci, *What We May Be: Techniques for Spiritual Growth through Psychosynthesis* (New York: Tarcher, 2009).

Association for the Advancement of Psychosynthesis: www.aap-psychosynthesis.org.

Dirk Kelder's psychosynthesis resource lists: articles and internet links: http://www.two.not2.org (accessed June 26, 2011).

Douglas Russel, "Seven Basic Constructs of Psychosynthesis," *Psychosynthesis Digest*, vol. 1, no. 2, (Spring–Summer 1982): http://two.not2.org/psychosynthesis/articles/pd1-2.htm (accessed June 2011).

Further Reading Resources on the Soul

Gary Zukav, *The Seat of the Soul* (New York: Fireside, 1990).

Stephen Mitchell, *Bhagavad Gita: A New Translation* (New York: Three Rivers Press, 2000).

Michael Newton, *Journey of Souls* (St. Paul: Llewellyn Publications, 1994).

Janet Conner, *Writing Down Your Soul: How to Activate and Listen to the Extraordinary Voice Within* (San Francisco: Conari Press, 2008).

Appendix C

Suggestions for Psychotherapists: Using the Eight Steps to Freedom with Your Clients

This method will not be appropriate for all of your clients. It is not appropriate to use with a client with a personality disorder, in a state of active addiction, or in a state in which emotional destabilization will cause the person to turn to self-destructive behaviors.

This method will be useful for your clients who are:
- Self-aware and self-regulating
- Grounded in a basic sense of their identities
- Capable of studying and learning a technique
- Able to use their own wills as tools for change
- In a trusting relationship with their Higher Powers
- Comfortable sharing their emotions with you, their therapist
- Framing their therapy work as a forgiveness issue

Your clients are ready to forgive when:
- They have vulnerably touched the emotional pain of their wounds and shared it with you honestly.

- They have grown tired of the archaic patterns their stories are causing in their present lives, and they ask, *Now what? How do I move on from this?*
- They have examined and gained insight about what decisions they made, or what limiting beliefs about life, self, or others they took on because of their wounds.
- They have been educated about what forgiveness is, and how the method works to bring completion to this issue.
- They are open to working with a Higher Power, a spiritual source of healing and renewal.

Sometimes we have to do some preparatory work with a client to help him or her "make friends" with the concept of forgiveness. For some people, Step One (State Your Will to Make a Change) is the biggest challenge of all, because they first have to work through their prior attitudes about forgiveness, and learn about what real forgiveness is *not*. They need to be helped to understand that forgiveness is *not*: excusing or approving the wrong behavior of the offender, forgetting that the offensive incident occurred, allowing further abuse, reconciling with the offender, or giving up on what is appropriate for them.

It is helpful if your clients listen to or read about inspiring examples of the empowering relief of forgiveness, in order to understand that forgiveness is something they will do for their own sakes, and it will free them to move forward. We must kindle in the clients some faith in a modality of healing that has helped many people find permanent relief from painful issues. I also recommend that you invite your clients to create a joyful vision of themselves that they can move toward in the foreseeable future.

Once a client has successfully integrated Step One, the client-therapist team may choose to work through the issues in a systematic way—make a list, do some preparatory homework, and clear through each issue one by one, from easiest to most difficult—or in an organic fashion, working through the parts and pieces of issues as they present themselves, session by session (Steps Two and Three). Eventually, the client will have the confidence to bring herself to the healing of the painful core of her issue, utterly transforming her self-concept and capability to choose and create a different and better future.

There are two important imperatives for the therapist who intends to make our forgiveness method a potent and reliable tool in his or her therapy toolbox. First, the therapist must be comfortable with seeking a shared understanding of the client's own spiritual framework, agreeing on the spiritual imagery and language that the team will use. Together, the client and therapist must be able to appeal to the presence and help of a Higher Power, a spiritual source that will assist the client in transforming his or her past, present, and future. (This is key in Steps Four, Five, Six, and Seven.) Most clients are willing to utilize the imagery of light and love coming from a Source that is beyond them, sending healing energy down into their personalities through the crown of the head. This transpersonal energy restores their boundaries, cleans out the debris from old expectations, and brings them into "right relationship" with self, other, and life itself. This transformation empowers them to "see the good" in their stories, because they can now access the wisdom inherent in the journey from being wounded to becoming whole again (Step Eight).

The second imperative for success is the therapist's personal familiarity with the experience of the Eight Steps to Freedom, because he or she has successfully used this method to resolve persistent personal issues a number of times. This experience informs the therapist's skill and intuition as a facilitator of forgiveness, and inspires faith and confidence in the client who is seeking the healing resolution of a long-held inner conflict.

There is little that is more rewarding or more of a privilege than facilitating the experience of forgiveness for another person. At a certain point in the journey through the Eight Steps, there comes a pivotal moment of change, when the former struggle melts away, and the psyche becomes newly established in the "now," with all of its fresh possibilities. This moment is a bonding and liberating experience for client and therapist alike, and a significant turning point in the therapy process.

Appendix D

The Eight Steps to Freedom and the Twelve-Step Recovery Program: Partners in Transforming Dysfunction to Serenity

Learning how to forgive, in real terms, significantly empowers one's recovery program. In fact, we can say that the process of forgiving self and others is *central* to the Twelve-Step Program. The Eight Steps to Freedom and the self-forgiveness exercise are a perfect adjunct to the Twelve Steps of Alcoholics Anonymous. They empower this time-tested recovery path by bringing new clarity to the steps that some have termed "the muddle in the middle," thus accelerating the process of healing the dysfunctional past. These methods provide a way to methodically clear up the pain and heaviness from past resentments and mistakes, which are partly to blame for the chronic urge to use drugs or alcohol.

If you take a step back and observe the Twelve Steps in several larger chunks, you can see that the first three steps are about starting a good relationship with a Higher Power, the middle steps have to do with forgiveness and cleaning up the past, and the later steps help us to deepen our spirituality and build new integrity into daily life. I will briefly list the Twelve Steps, followed by a closer look at Steps Four to Ten, which are about forgiveness.

The Twelve Steps of Alcoholics Anonymous

Step One: Admitted we were powerless over alcohol, that our lives had become unmanageable.

Step Two: Came to believe that a Power greater than ourselves could restore us to sanity.

Step Three: Made a decision to turn our will and our lives over to the care of God as we understood Him.

Step Four: Made a searching and fearless moral inventory of ourselves.

Step Five: Admitted to God, to ourselves, and to another human being the exact nature of our wrongs.

Step Six: Were entirely ready to have God remove all these defects of character.

Step Seven: Humbly asked Him to remove our many shortcomings.

Step Eight: Made a list of all persons we had harmed, and became willing to make amends to them all.

Step Nine: Made direct amends to such people wherever possible, except when to do so would injure them or others.

Step Ten: Continued to take personal inventory, and when we were wrong promptly admitted it.

Step Eleven: Sought, through prayer and meditation, to improve our conscious contact with God as we understood Him, praying only for knowledge of His will for us and the power to carry that out.

Step Twelve: Having had a spiritual awakening as the result of these steps, we tried to carry this message to alcoholics, and to practice these principles in all our affairs.

The AA Steps that Are Related to Forgiveness

Step Four: Made a searching and fearless moral inventory of ourselves.

We are encouraged to make a list of our resentments toward others, as well as our mistakes and character defects. This is a very difficult step, but recovery is not possible without it. Step Four makes us face our shame, guilt, anger, grief, and regrets, because those are the things that are keeping us sick and feeding the overwhelming power of our addictions. We identify our forgiveness issues: those toward others and those toward ourselves. We now have a list that we can work through methodically, releasing old hurts and resentments toward others, one by one. Each time we forgive someone on our inventory list, we drain away some of the emotional reactivity that tempts us to use alcohol or another substance, and we install more Higher Power energy and connection within our body/mind.

Step Five: Admitted to God, to ourselves, and to another human being the exact nature of our wrongs.

We put an end to denial and isolation and aloneness. We get together with another person, and with them and God as our witnesses, we speak aloud the details of the actions and the attitudes that have caused so much shame and destruction within us and around us during our using years. We put it all out on the table honestly.

Steps Six and Seven: Were entirely ready to have God remove all these defects of character. Humbly asked Him to remove our shortcomings.

We express our willingness to live in a new and better way, and to allow God to remove our problems and character defects. We clearly ask Him to do this for us. The Self-Forgiveness Exercise taught in this book is a technique that combines Step Six and Step Seven, and gives you a practical way of accomplishing these steps. If you need to, you just make the translation of "self-forgiveness" to mean "Higher Self (God) forgiveness" of the personal self, and you will accomplish the release that Steps Six and Seven are all about.

Steps Eight and Nine: Made a list of all persons we had harmed, and became willing to make amends to them all. Made direct amends to such people wherever possible, except when to do so would injure them or others.

We give ourselves a chance to apologize to others and request their forgiveness, if it is appropriate for us to do this with them. This step is so much easier to do if you have already forgiven yourself for your harmful actions. It's easier to make those phone calls and have those awkward meetings with people in your life, if you have already faced and cleared out the deep shame you felt about hurting them when you were out of control. In other words, if God has already forgiven you, what power do others hold over you if they choose to remain unforgiving? You can make peace with yourself and your past whether other people are able to help you do so or not.

Step Ten: Continued to take personal inventory, and when we were wrong promptly admitted it.

We are encouraged to stay honest and realistic about our behavior, and promptly make an adjustment when we are off the mark. Here again, self-forgiveness is so valuable in giving us the courage to face our disappointing behaviors and still love ourselves unconditionally. When we tap into the vast reservoir of patience and encouragement that exists in our Higher Power, we become willing to admit our failings and dust ourselves off each day as we make a decision to do better tomorrow.

Prevent Relapse by Using the Eight Steps to Freedom

The disease of addiction has been declared "cunning, baffling, and powerful." It is often a tangled knot of tendencies that arise out of one's ancestry and genetics, post-traumatic stress from untreated trauma, physical allergy, and stubborn subpersonalities that function as psychological defense systems. The complexity of this disease accounts for why most addicts must make healing from addiction a lifelong concern, and recovery practices a lifelong habit. Chief among the obstacles to recovery is the common tendency to have a messy relapse into the disease behavior, which renews more of the attendant shame and hopelessness the person was struggling with in the first place.

Relapse prevention has many components to it, and one of the best ways a person in recovery can progress and prevent relapse is to utilize the Eight Steps to Freedom to heal latent emotional problems. The old, untreated emotional wounds created the psychological pressure that triggers the desire to use a substance. On the path of recovery, the work of healing old wounds and resentments and forgiving one's self for the dysfunction of the past and present is absolutely necessary in order to get us onto new ground in our life and be able to stay there, building a new story for the future.

Appendix E

Current Research on Forgiveness and Health

Glenn Affleck, Howard Tennen, Sydney Croog, and Sol Levine, "Casual Attribution, Perceived Benefits, and Morbidity after a Heart Attack: An 8-Year Study," *Journal of Consulting and Clinical Psychology*, 55, no. 1 (1987): 29–35.

Norah C. Feeny, Lori A. Zoellner, and Edna B. Foa, "Anger, Dissociation and Posttraumatic Stress Disorder among Female Assault Victims," *Journal of Traumatic Stress*, 13, no. 1 (2000): 89–100.

S. R. Freedman and R. D. Enright, "Forgiveness as an Intervention Goal with Incest Survivors," *Journal of Consulting and Clinical Psychology*, 64, no. 5 (1996): 983–92.

Alex H. S. Harris and Carl E. Thoresen, "Forgiveness, Unforgiveness, Health, and Disease," in *Handbook of Forgiveness*, ed. Everett L. Worthington, Jr. (New York: Routledge, 2005).

Kathleen A. Lawler, Jarred W. Younger, Rachel L. Piferi, Eric Billington, Rebecca Jobe, Kimberly A. Edmondson, and Warren H. Jones, "A Change of Heart: Cardiovascular Correlates of Forgiveness in Response to Interpersonal Conflict," *Journal of Behavioral Medicine*, 26, no. 5 (2003): 373–93.

Kathleen A. Lawler, Jarred W. Younger, Rachel L. Piferi, Rebecca L. Jobe, Kimberly A. Edmondson, and Warren H. Jones, "The Unique Effects of Forgiveness on Health: An Exploration of Pathways," *Journal of Behavioral Medicine*, 28, no. 2 (2005): 157–67.

James Murray, Anke Ehlers, and Richard A. Mayou, "Dissociation and Post-Traumatic Stress Disorder: Two Prospective Studies of Road Traffic Accident Survivors," *British Journal of Psychiatry*, 180 (2002): 363–68.

Robert M. Sapolsky, "The Physiology and Pathophysiology of Unhappiness," in *Handbook of Forgiveness*, ed. Everett L. Worthington, Jr. (New York: Routledge, 2005).

Robert M. Sapolsky, *Why Zebras Don't Get Ulcers*, 3rd ed. (New York: Henry Holt and Company, 2004).

Howard Tennen and Glenn Affleck, "Blaming Others for Threatening Events," *Psychological Bulletin*, 108, no. 2 (1990): 209–32.

Loren Toussaint and John L. Webb, "Theoretical and Empirical Connections between Forgiveness, Mental Health, and Well-Being," in *Handbook of Forgiveness*, ed. Everett L. Worthington, Jr. (New York: Routledge, 2005).

Bessel A. Van der Kolk, "Adolescent Vulnerability to Posttraumatic Stress Disorder," *Journal for the Study of Interpersonal Processes*, 48, no. 4 (1985): 365–70.

Martina A. Waltman, "The Psychological and Physiological Effects of Forgiveness Education in Male Patients with Coronary Artery Disease," *Dissertation Abstracts International: Section B: The Sciences and Engineering*, 63, no. 8-B (2003): 3971.

C. V. O. Wilvliet, K. A. Phipps, M. E. Feldman, and J. C. Beckham, "Posttraumatic Mental and Physical Health Correlates of Forgiveness and Religious Coping in Military Veterans," *Journal of Traumatic Stress*, 17, no. 3 (2004): 269–73.

Appendix F

Notes on the Subtle Energy System

One of the things that distinguishes the Eight Steps to Freedom from other methods of forgiveness is the acknowledgment and utilization of the subtle energy system for healing an emotional wound and its residue in the body. The physical refreshment that comes with the experience of forgiveness is due to the release of old, "stuck" energy in the body, and the restoration of a flow of healthy new energy. The relative health of the "flow" of life force in the subtle energy body may well be the key to the physical body being able to remain vital and free of disease.

Although Western medicine has been slow to acknowledge this idea, or even the very existence of the subtle energy body, it has long been acknowledged by other ancient systems of medicine—Chinese and Indian Ayurvedic—and the model of the chakra system is widely acknowledged today in the alternative/complementary therapies that have grown up independently of standard Western medicine. There are a number of sophisticated works on the subtle body (see "Further Reading Resources" below), but for our purposes in the Eight Steps, I present here a simple synthesis that highlights the features you need to know for a successful forgiveness experience. The keys to understanding how to recognize and use the resource of your subtle body for healing are found in the concepts of:

1. Our *sources* of vital energy

2. The healthy *circulation* of energy throughout the body in the chakra system

3. The healthy energy *boundary*, or aura, in our environment and with people

Our Sources of Vital Energy

We receive energy from above, below, and all around us. Life-giving energy comes from below us, from the green vitality of the planet Earth, which supports the health of every creature in every ecosystem of the biosphere. Human beings are mammals, and so, like every other animal, we have our "grounding"—the foundation of our physical nature. Our subtle energy systems have "roots" that extend into the ground a foot or so to an energy formation beneath the surface, our grounding center. This center is connected to the source of being and consciousness in the very heart of the Earth itself. Our roots draw energy from under the ground into our feet and legs, and up into the lower half of our torsos to feed the main energy system. Like sap rising in a trunk of a tree, energy flows upward into our beings, continually bringing biological renewal.

You also receive energy from above, from your soul, or Higher Self, which exists as a distinct energy entity within the vast ocean of Self—which you might think of as God or the Universe, depending on your framework. This eternal spark of conscious Universal Light is your personal connection, your gateway to the healing love/light/energy and creativity of that great Self. Your soul "plugs in" to your personality and its subtle energy body at a center twelve to eighteen inches over your head, which is known as the "transpersonal chakra." This large chakra is like a "step-down capacitor" between the unimaginable energy of the Creator and your own limited capacity as a human being to relate to that energy. For our purposes in conducting a successful forgiveness experience, it does not actually matter whether you believe that there is, in fact, an invisible sphere of light and healing energy hovering above your head, or whether you think of it as a creative visualization, a symbolic device of the mind that you use to call upon its healing resources. What matters is that, with some amount of faith and trust, you can reach to a source of healing above you that is beyond the limitations of your personality. You can clearly sense or imagine that you are able to open up a window of sorts at the very top of your head, and bring the love/light/energy from that source above you, down into your subtle and physical bodies—thus dissolving the energy block that has been troubling you.

The Healthy Circulation of Energy in the Chakra System

A *chakra*, a Sanskrit word meaning "wheel," is a swirling vortex that spins energy from the Universe into our personal beings. In the same way that the heart pumps blood through the veins and arteries of our physical bodies, the chakras move energy through the various channels of our subtle energy bodies. These channels have been called *meridians* in Chinese medicine and *nadis* in Indian philosophy. Like the in breath and the out breath, the inward-and-outward spiraling motion of the chakras draws energy in to nourish our beings. It also expresses our personal energy outward into our personal spaces, our auric fields. The health of each chakra center in the subtle energy system influences the glandular health of that area of the body, and the vibrancy of the body overall.

The seven main chakras are located in a line extending from the base of the torso to the top of the head, and they open to both the front and the back of the body. They are fed with energy from the transpersonal chakra above the head (where the eternal soul joins the personal self) and the transpersonal chakra below the ground (where the mortal personal self roots into the planet and participates in earthly life). There are many more minor chakras in the energy system, but we don't need to study those to accomplish forgiveness. The spinning motion of each chakra is part of the "distribution system" that delivers energy throughout our subtle bodies and into our physical bodies.

Alternative/complementary healing practitioners agree that unhealed wounds are held as blocks in the chakras, and these blocks eventually may cause physical health difficulties. Certain emotional issues also express themselves in specific chakras. Therefore, your awareness of your wound in your subtle body may have symptoms like heaviness, ache, blockage, or cold emptiness at the corresponding area of your physical body. Everyday examples of this abound: the "heavy heart," the "knife in your back," the "lump in your throat," and the sick feeling in your solar plexus when you feel shame or are being overpowered by another person's will. If you went to your family doctor and said, "Doctor, my heart is very heavy, something's wrong," he would not be able to see your problem with an x-ray, CAT scan, or MRI. It's in the subtle energy body, and we don't yet have the medical equipment to show these things (although a lab at UCLA has successfully recorded the *sound* of the chakras spinning at their classical locations on the body).

When you perform the Eight Steps to Freedom, the subtle energy system is apparent and important. In Step Two (Express Your Feelings), you accelerate your process of emotional release when you attempt to contact your emotions and speak their truth from the part of your body that feels heavy or blocked. In Step Four (Restore Your Boundaries), you restore the integrity of your personal space and visualize your aura as strong and whole. In Step Five (Open Up to the Universe to Get Your Needs Met in a Different Way), you open your seventh chakra like a big window and receive love/light/energy from the transpersonal chakra above your head into your subtle and physical bodies. You consciously move that energy down through you from head to toe, especially bringing concentrations of cleansing energy to the specific chakra(s) that were blocked with the old pain. When you send your love/light/energy from this transpersonal chakra through you and out to the person you've forgiven, you establish yourself in "right relationship" to him or her, whether the person is near or far, alive or passed away. It is during the journey of Steps Four, Five, and Six that your aura is truly "repaired" and you establish stronger energetic boundaries with the person you've forgiven, and similar people, from then on. At the end of the Eight Steps, you can consciously identify the nature of the healing that occurred, in part, by the discernable sense of lightness in one or more of your chakra centers.

The chakras and related personality issues:

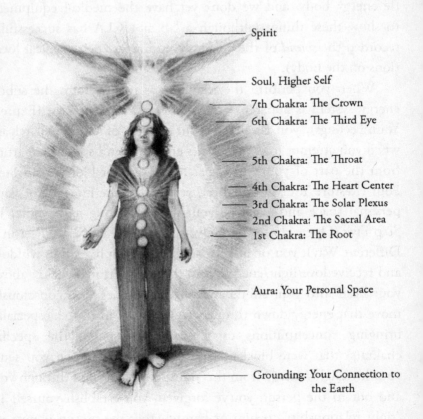

Spirit

Soul, Higher Self

7th Chakra: The Crown

6th Chakra: The Third Eye

5th Chakra: The Throat

4th Chakra: The Heart Center

3rd Chakra: The Solar Plexus

2nd Chakra: The Sacral Area

1st Chakra: The Root

Aura: Your Personal Space

Grounding: Your Connection to the Earth

The Subtle Energy System

The chakras distribute the light and energy of Spirit and the nourishing vitality of planet Earth throughout the subtle energy body. The energy body nourishes the health and vitality of your physical body.

First: The root chakra

- Tailbone, the base of the spine

- Grounding, physical comforts, physical and financial survival, security, ancestral heritage, and relationship to the Earth

Second: The sacral chakra
- Between pubis and navel; includes generative and elimination organs
- Gender identification, sexuality, bonding with a mate, fertility, and creativity

Third: The solar plexus
- Stomach region
- Power, safety, personal space, will, common sense, reality, individuation, and self-esteem

Fourth: The heart center
- Heart, chest cavity
- Love, connectivity, joy, hope, devotion, sharing, compassion, belonging, and community
- This chakra is considered the most important, the "bridge" between the earthly personality and the soulful self

Fifth: The throat
- Seat of expression
- Truth, knowledge, discrimination, service, humility, and self-expression

Sixth: The third eye
- Center of the forehead
- Purpose, vision, planning, synthesis, integration, self-realization, and unity consciousness

Seventh: The crown
- Top of the head
- God-realization, relationship to God and the Universe, Divine guidance and inspiration, and the doorway to universal energy and healing

The Healthy Energy Boundary, or Aura, in Our Environment and with People

The aura, your personal energetic space, is visible to some people with sensitive sight as a field of light around the body, especially visible around the head. It is both an expression of the energy within you shining out into the space around you and a protective sheath that enables you to filter out worldly and personality energies that might otherwise overwhelm your will or your senses. On a psychological level, the strength of the aura is determined by the strength and integrity of the healthy ego—the sense of an intact, whole *self* that walks through life with attitudes of trust, goodwill, high self-esteem, and innate self-worth. All of these attitudes function together as a protection of sorts in social situations.

If you grew up with a lack of support for your healthy individuality, or were hurt by your caregivers instead of being nurtured and helped by them, you may have a weak, partial, or permeable auric field, which is a true health problem in your subtle energy body. It can cause you to be easily intimidated or overwhelmed by personalities with more will and energy, and quickly tired out in high-energy situations like parties or the shopping mall. Your aura can be consciously strengthened and brought to full health with energy healing, assertiveness training, visualization, and especially forgiveness work with the Eight Steps to Freedom. Every time you forgive a person who overwhelmed you, weakened you, or took advantage of your weakness in the past, you reclaim your personal space and rebuild it with new energy that increases your serenity and confidence.

Further Reading

Barbara Brennan, *Hands of Light: A Guide to Healing Through the Human Energy Field* (New York: Bantam Books, 1988).

Caroline Myss, *Anatomy of the Spirit: The Seven Stages of Power and Healing* (New York: Three Rivers Press, 1996).

Bruce Burger, *Esoteric Anatomy: The Body as Consciousness* (New York: North Atlantic Books, 1998).

Betsy Rippentrop and Eve Adamson, *The Complete Idiot's Guide to Chakras* (New York: Alpha, 2009). (Author note: despite the title, this book is excellent—simple but comprehensive.)

Anodea Judith *Wheels of Life: A User's Guide to the Chakra System* (St. Paul: Llewellyn Publications, 2010).

Cyndi Dale, *The Subtle Body: An Encyclopedia of Your Energetic Anatomy* (Boulder: Sounds True, 2009).

Appendix G

Eight Steps to Freedom: Quick Reference

The Personality Blocked by Resentment

When you have an unresolved wound, it is stuck in your energy body. It impacts your physical health and blocks a clear connection to your soul.

Prepare for a Change in Your Life

Arrange some time, in a private place, and enlist support from someone you trust.

STEP ONE: State Your Will to Make a Change

Say out loud your determination to let go now and heal your wound
completely.

STEP TWO: Express Your Feelings Exactly as They Are inside You

Speak out your emotional truths; "vent" and release them physically if necessary.

STEP THREE: Release Expectations from Your Mind, One by One

Shift the expectation to a positive preference: "I prefer that you ..." or "I wish ..."

Acknowledge reality, and restate your will to move on.

Release this expectation with definitive words and a gesture.

Imagine this block inside you dissolving and new space opening up within.

Do this process with each expectation you have.

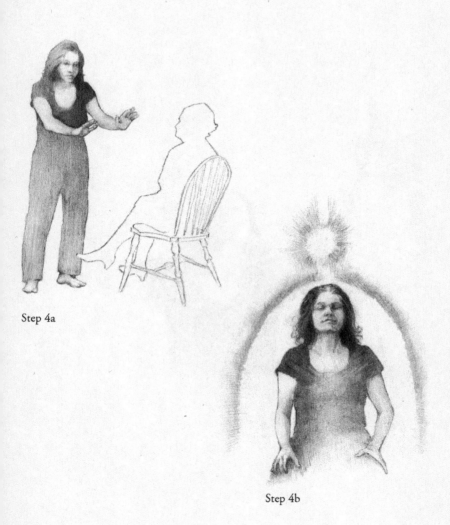

Step 4a

Step 4b

STEP FOUR: Restore Your Boundaries

Give the person you're forgiving full responsibility for his or her actions and attitudes.

Visualize your healthy personal space, filled with your own light.

STEP FIVE: Open up to the Universe to Get Your Needs Met in a Different Way

The Universe wants you to thrive!

STEP SIX: Receive Spirit's Healing Energy into Your Personality

Open up your crown center and bring love and light from above you down into your personality, cleansing the body, soothing the heart and feelings, and bringing peace to the mind. Imagine this fresh new energy pouring into your subtle energy body too.

STEP SEVEN: Send Unconditional Love to the Other Person and Release Him or Her

Imagine sending rays of love and light to the person, just as he or she is; say, "I send you this higher love, just as you are. I release you, and I release myself from you."

STEP EIGHT: See the Good in the Person or Situation

Say what is good about the person, or what you have learned in this situation.

Integrate Your Change

Take some time to rest, to think, to be; start living in a new way.

Appendix H

The Soul-Illumined Personality:
Daily Centering Exercise

The following is an exercise that will fortify and reinforce your healthy personal space; you can use it for specific occasions when you need to be strong, or do it as a daily exercise that will build on itself over time to give you good boundaries every day.

The Soul-Illumined Personality

You are an eternal soul in a human personality. The Creator's Light dwells with you as your Higher Self.

Daily Centering Exercise

1. **Call yourself here** to the present when you wake up in the morning. Say your own name in a strong voice. Sing or hum a song you love.

2. **Ground yourself to planet Earth.** Imagine roots or cords sprouting down from your feet to the fiery core of planet Earth. Imagine the Earth's strong, nurturing energy rising up through your feet and legs to the bottom of your spine (root chakra), anchoring you. Affirm this: "I am _____ (your name), grounded in the Earth."

3. **Contain yourself.** Visualize in front of you a container for your spiritual energy that looks just like your physical body—a glass statue of yourself. Slip it on like a second skin. Pause to remember that you will take responsibility for all of your own feelings and intentions today. Affirm this: "I am _____, contained within myself."

4. **Protect yourself.** Picture your aura around you like a bubble that is strong and firm. Instruct yourself that your aura will allow you to share positive, life-giving energy with others and filter out unwanted influences. Breathe into your space, and imagine your breath fills it with your own colored light. Affirm this: "I am _____, open but protected."

5. **Open up the channel to guidance and intuition.** Imagine a clear "pipeline" that extends from the top of your head, at your crown chakra, upward to the light of your soul, located at the transpersonal chakra (twelve to eighteen

inches overhead). Your soul and this chakra are connected to the vast wisdom of God and/or the Universe. Tell your soul that you are open to guidance and intuition that will help you experience the best day possible, and ask it to bring to you throughout the day everything you need for safety and happiness. Affirm this: "I am _____, open to guidance and intuition for my safety and happiness."

6. **State your present intentions.** Invoke your intelligent will to create what you want for each day: it might be an attitude, an experience, or the accomplishment of certain short-term or long-term goals. Be clear about what's important to you today and say it out loud. Then walk forward and stay present, with your intuition open and your boundaries intact. You will amaze yourself with your new ease and productivity! State your affirmation, such as "Today I will easily finish my school paper," "Today I will be open to sharing the best that's in me with my spouse," or "Today I will remain in the goodness of the present moment."

7. **Picture yourself going through your day with your personal space intact, fulfilling your intentions.** Imagine yourself going through your upcoming meeting or workday with your roots into the ground, your own energies contained, your mind open to wisdom and intuition, and your aura shielding you from unnecessary distraction, as you fulfill your intentions. Clearly visualize yourself at your best. Affirm this: "Today I will operate as my best self. I am _____, grounded, contained, and protected. I am open to guidance and intuition as I gracefully fulfill my intentions."

8. **Check in with yourself** a few times during the day. Are you contained? Have you lost your grounding? Can you empty your mind and listen "up" with your intuition? Renew the integrity of your personal space especially before and after events that trigger anxiety for you. Remember your intentions. If you've lost your boundaries or your intentions, notice what stimulus made you lose it, and make notes to do some self-healing around this issue.

9. **At the end of the day, clear your personal space.** Notice what concerns you have taken on that are not yours. Breathe them away. Notice what people and problems you carried along with you that you need to detach from. Give them full responsibility for themselves. Notice what you've accomplished and feel grateful about. Release your expectations about anything that remains undone. Go to bed with a clean mind after your masterful day!

Finish each day and be done with it.
You have done what you could.

Some blunders and absurdities have crept in;
forget them as soon as you can.

Tomorrow is a new day.
You shall begin it serenely and with too high a spirit
to be encumbered with your old nonsense.

—RALPH WALDO EMERSON

Meet **Mary Hayes Grieco**, director and lead trainer of The Midwest Institute for Forgiveness Training in Minneapolis, Minnesota (USA). The Midwest Institute provides forgiveness training programs for the general public, for counseling professionals, and for committed students of self-mastery, who are shedding the past and going to a new level of purposefulness. In this video, you will step into the public forgiveness workshop to get a feel for its supportive community atmosphere as well as Mary's joyful exuberance as she shares her life work with the group. You will also hear the testimonials of two participants who have found freedom with this forgiveness method. Further resources are available at www.forgivenesstraining.com.